LOST *in the*

★ ★ ★ ★ **Victory**

Reflections of
American War Orphans
of World War II

LOST in the

★ ★ ★ ★ Victory

*Reflections of
American War Orphans
of World War II*

collected by

Susan Johnson Hadler and Ann Bennett Mix

edited by

Calvin L. Christman

University of North Texas Press

Denton, Texas

The paper in this book meets the minimum requirements of the American National Standard for Permanence of Paper for Printed Library Materials, Z39.48.1984.

Permissions
University of North Texas Press
PO Box 311336
Denton TX 76203-1336
940-565-2142

Library of Congress Cataloging-in-Publication Data

Lost in the victory: reflections of American war orphans of World War II / collected by Susan Johnson Hadler and Ann Bennett Mix : Calvin Christman, editor.
p.   cm.
Includes index.
ISBN 1-57441-033-4 (alk. paper)
1. World War, 1939–1945—Children—United States. 2. Orphans—United States—Biography. I. Hadler, Susan Johnson, 1945–   . II. Mix, Ann Bennett, 1940–   . III. Christman, Calvin L.

D810.C4L64   1998   97-26872
940.53'161—dc21   CIP

Design by Accent Design and Communications
Proceeds from this book will be donated to the AWON

Dedicated to two soldiers who did not return from World War II and to one sailor who did:

Sydney Worthington Bennett (1919–1945)

David Selby Johnson, Jr. (1919–1945)

Herbert Emanuel Christman (1908–   )

Contents

Editor's Note

*O*ne of my first memories came when my father returned from Okinawa in November 1945. I was a few months past my third birthday and recall clearly that Dad came home wearing his gray navy khaki uniform. In addition, he had added a moustache since I had seen him last. Shaving that moustache was one of his first actions upon his arrival back home, and I remember quite clearly standing next to him, with my small hands tightly gripping the washstand, looking up at this wonderful man as he shaved. To this day, it remains my most precious early memory.

Thousands of American wartime children have no such memory. Their fathers never returned. Their loss made up part of the terrible cost of World War II, a loss made more difficult by the fact that, as the nation celebrated its victory and hastened to embrace a world without war, this price of battle went largely unnoticed and forgotten. I am an example of this flawed vision and memory. Until Ann Mix of the American World War II Orphans Network (AWON) contacted me, I had not given even a passing consideration of what might have happened if my dad had not returned from the Pacific. After all, he came home. I *knew* he came home. And without any conscious thought, I simply projected my own small individual experience to the other sons and daughters of the warriors of World War II.

Ann's phone call scratched hard at my memory and conscience. It forced me to consider what our family's life would have been if my dad had not come back. The picture was terrifying. My Mother would have had to care for three children—at that time, ages three, eight, and nine—and her own mother—permanently bedridden with a paralytic stroke and polio. One of those children would soon develop diabetes. Gone would have been her husband and our father, the promising young physician who had volunteered for service after Pearl Harbor, and the future chief of medicine of a large suburban hospital of Cleveland. Missing would have been the love and security he would give in such abundance. How terribly different life would have been for us. How terribly different life did become for so many American war orphans of World War II.

These pages hold the stories of some of those orphans. In the early 1990s, Susan Johnson Hadler and Ann Bennett Mix, both of whom had lost their fathers in April 1945, began collecting war orphan interviews, letters, family histories, clippings, poems, and photos, which are now part of the archives of AWON in Bellingham, Washington. Their work was a labor of love and healing. Although the stories in this volume are not enough from which to draw any final statistical lessons, the orphans' words represent a crucial beginning toward understanding their experience. Their chapters provide a clear, poignant, and essential snapshot of a part of World War II that, until now, has been both ignored and untold.

Calvin L. Christman
DeSoto, Texas

Preface

We were lost in the green hills of Tuscany searching for the American Military Cemetery near Florence where Ann's father is buried. "There's a man with white hair, old enough to remember the war." We pulled up beside him in our tiny rented Fiat. Referring to our Italian phrase books, we looked up the words one by one: cemetery, "cimitero"; where?, "dove"; "Americano." Now the words spilled out of Ann, "Mia padre muerto Italia guerra mondiale secondo." Ann would never have blurted out those words back home, where we learned not to speak of our fathers' deaths. But here in Italy people talked openly about the war. The man nodded as if it were ordinary conversation. "Si. Si." He pointed down the road and spoke too rapidly for us to find each word in our phrase books. "Grazie," we sang and drove off with renewed hope. After several more encounters with kind-hearted elderly Italians, we turned into the cemetery driveway and parked.

Ann was four years old when her father was shot and killed by the Germans in a medieval village on a mountain top in northern

Italy, April 19, 1945. One week earlier, my father had been blown to bits by a mine in Germany. I was three months old. My father's name is carved on the "Wall of Missing" at the American Cemetery in Luxembourg.

Both of us grew up knowing almost nothing about our fathers. Over the past half decade we sent for their military and mortuary records. We contacted war buddies, researched troop histories, dug for any information that shed light on our fathers, who they were and what happened to them. Help came from other war orphans, administrators, veterans, friends and relatives, as well as from the French, Italians, and Germans. No longer alone with our loss and our longings, we helped each other persevere and understand. All the help we received had now guided us to these cemetery gates.

We stopped on the stone bridge and looked across the stream to the vast green field that held the white marble markers of thousands of American soldiers who died in those three bloody years, 1943–1945. With each marker, we imagined a young man, the age now of our own sons. We saw each stone as once a son with a future, or once a husband, a father with a family. Beloved. Lost. We walked silently up the gravel path toward the orderly rows of crosses and Stars of David, passing the first several rows, reading the names as we turned down Row C, counting over to 34. "Sydney Worthington Bennett." Ann sat down on the soft grass that covers her father's grave. She touched the letters that spell his name. She talked quietly about her dad; his humor, the poems he wrote. He was still a kid who loved to play pool and drink beer. He smoked a pipe, and when he went to war in the spring of 1944, he left a wife and three children in Bakersfield, California.

Other fathers were buried here. Some were fathers of friends we met through the AWON who have never been able to visit these graves. Late in the afternoon we visited the graves of their fathers and took pictures to give them when we returned to the states and thought, too, of their losses.

*　　　*　　　*

In 1990, Ann Mix began her search to find out about her father. She met others whose fathers had been killed in World War II. Nearly everyone to whom she spoke longed to know more about their fathers. They wanted to talk about them and about their lives as war orphans. As a result, Ann founded the AWON in 1991. She began locating war orphans and gathering sources of information about servicemen who were fathers in World War II, material she shared with those who were also searching for information about their fathers. The more she spoke with other orphans, the clearer it became that they had stories that needed to be told; stories that had too long been cloaked by silence; stories marked with tragedy and resilience, pain and stoicism; and always stories of love for fathers who, barely known, were never forgotten, stories of a void that could neither be filled nor ignored.

Visiting the Vietnam Veteran's Memorial Wall on Veteran's Day, 1992, I felt the familiar loneliness of having no place to go to honor my father. I stopped to read a poem placed against the Wall and noted it was written by a child to her father. At that moment I realized there must be many of us across the country whose fathers had died in World War II. Some of them might be as isolated with their loss as I. Following the sad procession that day along the glistening black wall as it thickened with the names of the Vietnam War dead, I vowed to end the silence and to understand what had happened to our fathers and to those who have carried the sorrows of the nation's World War II losses.

My collaboration with Ann began when we discovered that we wanted to write the same book. We learned that there has been no attempt to document the number of children who were orphaned in World War II or to learn from their experiences. Records which could have helped sociologists, psychologists, and historians were not kept. There was almost no literature on American war orphans of World War II. Little had been written by the government, by society, or by our families. Our fathers and the void they left behind had rarely been mentioned, and we had never understood why. We began to interview war orphans, many of whom had joined the AWON. As children, they felt the awkwardness surrounding any mention of their fathers. They learned to keep quiet. It was only with great reticence even now that they talked with anyone about their losses and the impact on their lives. Their willingness to tell their stories has made this book possible.

The voices in this book are the voices of the sons and daughters who for half a century have seldom spoken of their fathers or of their own lives after the deaths of their fathers. These are the stories of those who were "lost in the victory" of World War II. The stories told here are filled with sadness and longing and love. They are stories remarkable for their honesty and their quiet courage in keeping the memories of their fathers alive. Publication of these stories breaks the silence and reminds us that many of the American soldiers who died in World War II were also fathers.

Susan Johnson Hadler
Washington, D.C.

Introduction

*W*e are American orphans of World War II. Most of us did not think of ourselves as orphans, even though we were fatherless. Like most people, we thought of war orphans as children in Europe or Asia who had lost both parents. We pictured a child in ragged clothes seated in the burnt-out rubble of a bombed building, a forlorn child wandering hungry and parentless through war-torn streets. World War II newsreels and magazine pictures showed us that war orphans lived overseas, not in the United States, where most of us had enough to eat and a place to live.

Since ancient times, fatherless children have been referred to as "orphans." In the United States, benefits paid to the fatherless children of war were given to widows and "orphans." Yet cultural ignorance of the existence of "war orphans" in this country goes so deeply that even those of us who are orphans are surprised by this description. Many will say, "I am not an orphan; I had my mother." Or "I don't think of myself that way." The dictionary, however, describes an orphan as a child who is bereft of one parent or both.

Near the end of the Civil War, in his Second Inaugural Address, Abraham Lincoln spoke of the dead soldier's child as "his orphan":

> With malice toward none; with charity for all; with firmness in the right, as God gives us to see the right, let us strive on to finish the work we are in; to bind up the nation's wounds; to care for him who shall have borne the battle, and for his widow, and his orphan—to do all which may achieve and cherish a just, and a lasting peace, among ourselves, and with all nations.

World War II orphans might find solace in Lincoln's words and in his recognition of our position. Yet the nation has largely ignored those thoughts. We were not cared for. We were not recognized. We were not even known. Our condition as "fatherless" was somehow to be magically fixed by a government check, a mother's remarriage, or a stepparent's adoption. What was our status? Who were we? We did not know. So, like society, we remained silent. We withdrew into our fears and fantasies, doing our best to ignore or accept our loss.

Historically, perhaps we should not have been surprised. Silence about the effects of war deaths on the families of survivors has traditionally been the norm both within those families and in the nation. Therese Rando, the author of one of the only references on war deaths, wrote that the World Federation for Mental Health in 1977 had noted:

> . . . after an exhaustive literature search and correspondence with the United States Department of Defense, investigators were stunned to find that no systematic studies on war bereavement were available or had ever been undertaken in the United States.[1]

American families who lost a loved one generally hid their suffering. With the arrival of a death-announcing telegram, silence descended like fog. As children, we absorbed the silence that enveloped our families, silence that usually obscured knowledge of our fathers and often negated awareness that we, as children, were affected by our fathers' deaths. Silence characterizes the war orphans' experience and intensifies their loss. The silence has continued for us into our adult lives. Most orphans rarely talked to their spouses or children about their experiences in relation to their fathers. They kept it to themselves and stayed alone with their memories and feelings, even though America immersed itself so deeply in World War II.

No government agency has a list of the American children whose fathers died in World War II. Nor do they have statistics on how many there were. Although benefits have been paid to individual dependents, no records were kept on the orphans themselves. After the children reached eighteen or finished schooling on the GI Bill, they disappeared from government records. There were no statistics on the number of war orphans.

The only estimate of the number of American children left fatherless by World War II comes from Department of Veterans Affairs' statistics on the number of dependents receiving benefits. Their records show the number of dependent children receiving benefits as a result of their fathers' deaths from all causes in World War II peaked at over 183,000.[2] This number, of course, does not include those dependents not receiving benefits because they did not apply for them or because the children were illegitimate.

When President Franklin D. Roosevelt signed the Selective Service Act on October 29, 1940, the law required the registration of all males between the ages of twenty-one and thirty-five and initiated America's first peacetime draft. Initially, the draft inducted only single men. After America entered the war, Congress lowered the minimum age to eighteen, although still continuing the exemption of married men.[3] The rise in wartime casualties and a concern that some men were using marriage as a means to escape service eroded support for this exemption. Brigadier General Lewis B. Hershey, who served as the director of Selective Service, declared in February 1942 that draft boards would assume ". . . that most of the recent marriages, contracted after the summer of 1941, might have been for the purpose of evading the draft. . . ."[4] By 1943, faced with the dilemma of drafting married men and fathers, Congress debated legislation to exempt fathers from the draft for the remainder of the war. However, it adjourned before passing the bill, and during its adjournment the Selective Service issued a decree removing the ban on inducting fathers. As of October 1, 1943, all married men with children were made eligible for the draft. This decree eliminated the Class III-A status: married with children.[5]

In October 1943, 13,000 fathers were drafted—6.8 percent of the total draftees for that month. By April 1944, slightly over half of all that month's inductees had children. Between October 1943 and December 1945, a total of 944,426 fathers were drafted, 30 percent of the total number drafted during those months. At the time Japan surrendered in September 1945, Selective Service classified 6,200,000 registrants as fathers, age 18 to 37. Of these, 20 percent were in active military service. The younger the father, the more likely he was to be in the military: more than half (58.2 percent) of the fathers in the age group 18 to 25 saw military duty.[6]

Too often, new batches of recruits were rushed through training, sent to replacement camps and into battle, where they died because of combat inexperience. Many of these recruits were fathers. Eugene Sledge, a veteran Marine on Okinawa, recalled that stream of replacements who " . . . came up confused, frightened and hopeful, got wounded or killed and went right back to the rear on the route by which they had come, shocked, bleeding or stiff."[7]

American society, influenced by the Victorian values of chastity, self sacrifice, and family nurturing, defined the lives of the women whom the war had widowed. Many women in the 1940s had minimal education, little training, and few job skills. They were unprepared to provide for themselves or for their children. Many young women moved in with relatives when their men left for the war. If the father were killed, many mothers with children found it necessary to prolong their stay. Some young widows never left their parents' homes again.

While wartime conditions were difficult for married women with children, unmarried mothers faced greater hardships and isolation. Illegitimacy occurred at a higher rate than normal during the war. The U.S. Census Bureau estimated that 650,000 illegitimate children were born in the United States during the war, with the greatest number coming in the latter part of the conflict.[8] Many other illegitimate births were not registered as such. Many women were pregnant by GIs who never intended to marry them or whom they never intended to marry. Ineligible to receive the soldiers' pay or survivors' benefits if the father were killed, mother and children were left to fend for themselves. Society judged women who had illegitimate children as immoral and often shunned them. Some women tried to protect themselves and the child by claiming they were married. Some unmarried mothers invented husbands and then declared them dead to explain their absence. Sometimes the status of the child's father was falsified to protect the father from undesired paternity. Grown children who had been told their fathers had died in the war would wonder about the absence of medals and flags or other mementos and about never having received benefits. In some cases, mothers found it necessary to put their children in orphanages or give them up for adoption.

On September 2, 1945, World War II ended with the surrender of Japan. Despite ticker tape parades in large cities, most of the men who survived drifted home without fanfare. The GIs arrived in their home towns quietly, on busses and trains. The returned soldiers, sailors, and airmen tried to pick up the pieces of their lives and forget the horrors of war. Although many men were badly damaged by their experiences, they received no counseling and rarely talked about what happened. They and their families were relieved the war was over and they were safe at home again. With or without adjustments, life would go on.

For most Americans, the postwar era was a time of prosperity. Houses were built with government loans, and veterans were educated on the GI Bill. The era introduced the age of television, automatic dishwashers, and electronic gadgets. Butter, sugar, meat, and shoes were readily available. People could drive anywhere; gasoline was cheap and plentiful, and tires had returned to the stores.

However, sprinkled throughout America were those who lost a son, a brother, an uncle or a friend. There were women who lost husbands and children who lost fathers. Among the thousands who died in the last months of the war, many were fathers, leaving their families in grief just as the nation celebrated victory.

It took several years to locate and rebury the bodies of many of the dead. Years after other families had gone on with their lives, some families were still attending burial ceremonies at private or national cemeteries. Widows were given the choice of leaving their husband's body overseas or having them returned to the United States. Some women chose to leave the body in a grave near the comrades with whom he died. Many women could not face the prospect of reopening their wounds by attending a burial, and decided to leave their husbands overseas. Of the 405,399 dead in the war, 93,242 were buried overseas, while a further 78,773 were missing or buried at sea.[9] Whatever the circumstances, the long-term result for the surviving children was that many were left with no nearby graves to visit, no place to be with their fathers spiritually, and no ceremonies to help them grieve. There was no complete closure for those families.

The government insurance money and the survivors' checks for the widows and orphans were seldom enough on which to live. Long before the term became widely used, orphans became "latch key" children while their mothers worked to support them. Many widows and their children relied on relatives for emotional and financial support. Some grandparents provided stability for fatherless children, especially when mothers were immobilized by problems adjusting to the deaths or working to rebuild lives. When grandparents died or insoluble conflicts led to family estrangements, war orphans experienced additional losses.

The young widows with children coped in a multitude of ways. Although their husbands' deaths left them bereft emotionally, financially, and physically, most were determined to do the best for their children. Many of these young women raised their children alone despite terrible hardships. Most of the fatherless families remained isolated and uncomplaining, without adequate resources, having to pretend everything was normal when very little was. The historian William M. Tuttle, in his study *Daddy's Gone to War*, reminds us that the constant admonition to the widow was, "If you can take it, your children can."[10]

With or without the "stiff upper lip," of course, some women simply could not deal with life after their husbands were killed. Some became alcoholic, some went insane, some killed themselves. The children of those mothers who never remarried often had to parent their mothers and themselves.

At best, it was hard for widows and orphans to "fit in" with the bustling family-oriented postwar society. Young mothers without husbands were often perceived as a threat by married women, and as needy by men. Remarriage helped to take away the stigma connected with being a war widow. Many widows remarried in haste to give themselves and their children the status and security they needed. Others were able to fall in love again.

The issue of remarriage posed a confusing dilemma for war orphans and their mothers. Many children whose mothers remained single wanted their mothers to remarry. When the mother did remarry, however, the children often had trouble accepting the stepfathers in place of their natural fathers. The introduction of a stepfather or the lack of a stepfather could profoundly affect the relationship between mother and child. Some children were neglected and some were badly abused by stepfathers who resented them. If there were no replacement father, or if the stepfather were not accepted as a replacement, the role of the father would often be assigned to the son or oldest daughter. This overburdened the children, tainted their relationships with their mothers, and often led to problems in their adult relationships. Occasionally the mother married a brother or a good friend of the child's father. In these situations, the father was openly remembered and the children were able to develop a picture of their father as a part of the family, leaving them with a greater sense of identity and wholeness.

Many World War II orphans knew almost nothing about their fathers. Many children were cut off from their paternal family members and from anyone who knew their dads, leaving them dependent on their mothers for knowledge of their fathers. Many of the mothers lost or destroyed pictures and mementos and memories of their children's fathers. Some, upon remarriage, changed their childrens' names. Sometimes this was done to force the children to accept their stepfathers as their true fathers and to normalize the child's life. Many children, however, resented their change of name, believing it destroyed their right to claim their fathers.

As children, we struggled against our mother's desire to forget and our own desire to remember. While many mothers needed to forget that painful episode in their young lives, we—the orphans—needed to know about our fathers. We are now in our fifties. We have completed our educations, raised our families, and established our careers. Now it is as if we are awakening from a dream in which our fathers were lost to us. We want to know who they were. Perhaps our awakening is occurring as we begin to face our own mortality and think about the linkage of our lives, the past and the future. We are beginning to ask the unanswered questions: How and where did our fathers die? Is there anyone who was with them when they died? Are there those who remember them? Are there pictures or letters to provide clues that can help us know our fathers? We are beginning to find the answers. We are beginning to realize how profoundly our lives have been affected by our losses. We want our children to know their grandfathers. We want to learn all we can before it is too late.

The attempt to get information about our fathers is difficult. For many of our mothers, questions open old wounds that are still too deep, too painful, too destructive. Or age has robbed them of the memory of our fathers and all that occurred so far away and long ago. They have nothing to tell us. Most of our fathers' parents have died, as have many of our fathers' friends and comrades. We seldom know people who knew our fathers. Government records are often the only links we have. Tragically for many of us, on July 12, 1973, a fire at the National Personnel Records Center in St. Louis, Missouri, where the government housed all the personnel records from World War II, destroyed approximately 80% of the records from the Army between 1912 and 1960. Of the 18 million records which survived, most were damaged. Only 2,800,000 of these have been reconstructed from other sources. Others will not be reconstructed unless someone requests them. The surviving files are rapidly turning brittle and soon will turn to dust. Other sources need to fill the gaps of our fathers' service.

In 1991, I founded the American World War II Orphans Network to help orphans search for information about their fathers by helping them send for military records, find family members with whom contact had been lost, locate war buddies who knew their fathers, and determine where their fathers were buried or in some way memorialized. Many orphans had never met another war orphan. Years of isolation end as we exchange information and support within the Network.

We are also coming together at last to grieve publicly and remember our fathers. In December 1991, "No Greater Love, "a national organization founded by Carmella Laspada that remembers the victims of war and terrorist attacks, held a memorial ceremony at Arlington National Cemetery for families of World War II casualties. For most of the families, it was the first ceremony and only "funeral" they had ever attended for their fathers and the first time they met others like themselves.

The stories in this anthology are told by those who lived them. This compilation of stories, however, by no means reflects the total experience of American World War II orphans. Missing from these stories is any account of the Afro-American, Asian-American, or Native American sons and daughters. Despite numerous attempts to locate children of these families, the search has been fruitless. The absence of their perspective is regretted. It is our hope that through this book some of these orphans will be found.

As we learn more about our fathers, remember them, and mourn them, we are beginning to free ourselves. Now we are able to reflect on our fathers and our lives as their orphans. Telling our stories is part of the restoration of our individual lost heritage. Beyond that, it is part of the unfinished work of the nation. William Tuttle in *Daddy's Gone to War* recalls the plight of American children caught in World War II.

> Children have never asked to be born into situations of war, and yet they repeatedly have been and they have suffered whether in the war zone or on the homefront. And it is because of adults' repeated mistakes that children, who understand war least, have been so deeply marked by it.[11]

His words merely add emphasis to the imperative expressed in those immortal words of Abraham Lincoln—"to bind up the nation's wounds"—and remind us of a duty no less necessary and proper today than it was in 1865. A combined effort must be made to care for all the widows and orphans left by the men who die in service to our country.

Ann Bennett Mix
Bellingham, Washington

[1] Therese A. Rando, *Treatment of Complicated Mourning* (Champaign, Illinois: Research Press, 1993), p. 520.
[2] *Annual Report of the Administrator of Veterans Affairs to the Congress for Fiscal Year 1957*, p. 242.
[3] William M. Tuttle, Jr., *"Daddy's Gone to War": The Second World War in the Lives of America's Children* (New York: Oxford University Press, 1993), p. 31.
[4] As quoted in Tuttle, p. 20.
[5] Tuttle, p. 31.

[6] Tuttle, p. 31.

[7] E. B. Sledge, *With the Old Breed at Peleliu and Okinawa* (Novato, CA: Presidio Press, 1990), p. 267.

[8] John Costello, *Virtue under Fire: How World War II Changed Our Social and Sexual Attitudes* (N.Y.: Fromm International Publishing, 1987), p. 203.

[9] American Battle Monuments Commission, *The American Battle Monuments Commission, World War II Commemorative Program* (1995), p. 2; U.S. Department of Defense, *Defense 89* (1989), p. 47; American Ex-Prisoners of War Association, *American Prisoners of War* (1990), p. 1.

[10] Tuttle, p. 45.

[11] Tuttle, p. 263.

Vince:
There Is a Part of Me Down Deep Which Never Heals

*V*incent C. Papke was an infantryman, serving in the 276th Regiment, 70th Division, in France. German fire had wounded him in January 1945, and he spent four weeks in a hospital before rejoining his unit in late winter. His death on March 4, 1945, came just over two months before the end of the European war. In a letter to Vincent's mother three months later, a regimental chaplain gave some details of her son's last day:

Vincent's death occurred about 8 o'clock in the morning, in the town of Stryring-Wendel [Stiring-Wendel, France], which is almost next door to the city of Forbach, a town near the French-German border. He was in a building along with a couple of other men, and stuck his head out of the window to give orders for covering fire for the squad. An enemy sniper shot him as he did so. He was wounded in the side, and I believe one of his lungs was punctured, but cannot say with certainty. His buddies rendered first aid and made Vincent as comfortable as they could while waiting for litter-bearers and an ambulance. Your son was very calm and courageous through it all. He asked for the picture of his wife which he carried in his wallet.

1

This was given him, and he died peacefully a few minutes later with the wallet in his hand.

Vincent Papke was twenty-nine years old when he died. He had been in the Army less than a year and had received two Purple Hearts and a Bronze Star. His son, Vincent, Jr., was then two-and-a-half years old.

The Papkes were a strong Catholic family. In fact, Vincent's chaplain in part of his letter noted that Vincent "was an outstanding Catholic, and most regular in his attendance at mass." Vincent, Jr., growing up in Richmond Hills, Queens, New York, served as an altar boy in his youth and attended Catholic schools. Although the family's religious belief gave them spiritual strength, it could not ameliorate the loss. Vincent, Jr., who today goes by "Vince," recalls:

The few photos, letters to my mom and his medals are all I have to remember him. These and a lifelong yearning and loneliness are the only memories of a father I longed to know.

My mom was devastated and fell into depression. My grandfather was unable to work for five years. The loss of my family continues to plague me all of my life. . . .

The War ended. My mom, a quiet and beautiful woman, went on with her life. She never dated and never remarried. Mom could not talk about what happened. My grandmother and grandfather would tell me about my dad. Mom eventually went to work so that I could go to parochial school. She worked for the U.S. Post Office and eventually developed brain cancer. She was sick for five years and finally left this world to be with her beloved spouse. I was their love child. It took my mom twenty-eight years of living alone to return to the peace of the Lord. Someday in the future, I will meet them, and they will hold me, and tell me that it's okay, and that nothing will ever separate us again.

Vince achieved an outstanding record as a youth. At his high school, LaSalle Academy, he helped lead his baseball team to a championship. His peers elected him both president of the senior class and student council president. In addition, he served as editor of the school newspaper. He went on to St. Johns' University on a combination Knights of Columbus and baseball scholarship. But for Vince, there was always the missing hand-shake or pat on the back from a father who never saw him score a game-winning run or heard him give a stirring student council speech.

Vince later joined the Marine Corps. "I suppose," he recalls, "that I felt that to die in a war was the only way to be like my dad." During a tour in Vietnam, however, he received a government order bringing him back to the United States when the Marine Corps learned that he was a sole sur-viving son of a veteran killed in war.

Ann Mix, founder of the AWON, first met Vince in 1991, in Washing-ton, D.C., at the "No Greater Love" ceremony that brought many war or-phans together for the first time. She recalled her conversation and impression:

Vince was wearing his father's two Purple Hearts. He was hand-some. He had a New York accent, and a slim, tanned, and hardened body disciplined by exercise. He wore a starched white shirt and white tennis shoes without one spot of dirt on them. His jeans were neatly creased and pressed. Yet, Vince talked about feeling out of control. He had recently been hospitalized for depression. He was still afraid and cried often.

Despite Vince's efforts to be perfect, he had failed in his own eyes. He had become alcoholic and was now in recovery. He had failed in his Catholic marriage, resulting in the divorce from his child-hood sweetheart. There had been four children. And, at times, he had been disabled with depression. Vince was finally beginning to understand how the loss of his father affected his family's life and his emotional stability.

In a later letter to Ann, Vince tried to grapple with his own emotions and memories:

There has not been a day that has gone by that I have not thought of my father and missed him. As a little boy, I watched all the war movies, again and again, crying like a baby. I watched them again, as a young man, with the same emotion, the same pain and the same longing. I thought for a long time that he had amnesia and would return home to be with me. I watched all of the WWII film clips, especially "Victory at Sea," hoping that I would spot him [on a troopship]; that he was still alive; that it was a terrible mistake. I played in our deserted attic alone, war games, that my father was alive and I had saved him! It never went away. I always missed him. I still miss him. He never saw me grow up; he's never seen my children. My grandmother's stories gave me a vision of a hero to look up to but I never met him. I never knew the strength of his support or the glow of his pride. I never felt the companionship that is shared only by a father and a son; there was no one sitting in the stands at my baseball games and no one to give me advice and love that only a father can give.

War destroys lives: it destroys families and changes the lives of those involved forever. It creates pain, pain which transcends and affects generations. It creates scars that can never heal. It will leave widows and orphans and bereaved parents who are never quite the same. It leaves fatherless children to grow up without the love, support and comfort of a father. It leaves wounds in the soul, wounds which can never be closed because the pain is too deep.

At the end of his neatly typed letter, Vince added a handwritten postscript:

I know I was loved and my children know I loved them, but there is a part of me down deep which never heals.[1]

[1]All material in AWON files.

Mr. and Mrs. Vincent C. Papke, 1940, Woodhaven, Long Island, New York.

Vincent Papke, Vincent Papke, Jr., and Arthur Beyer (in background). "My father and me—uncle in background—before he went away (his mom's backyard), Woodhaven, Long Island, New York. I was one-and-a-half years old. Notice his arms around me."

Vincent C. Papke at Fort Riley, Kansas, during the spring of 1944.

Vincent Papke, Jr., in Woodhaven in 1946.

Anne:

I Was Born in the Wake of Death

Anne's parents, Ed and Cecilia Moloney, were in their thirties when they married, although they had known each other since high school. They had been married four years and were living with her mother in Englewood, New Jersey, when Ed was drafted. When he left for the front, Cecilia was pregnant. Ed, a sergeant in the 273rd Infantry Regiment, 69th Infantry Division, was killed in Germany on April 14, 1945. He was thirty-five years old. Anne was born a month later.

Cecilia brought Anne home to the newborn's maternal grandmother. Anne refers to herself as the "first and the last," as her mother never remarried and she had no brothers or sisters. Her childhood family consisted of her mother and her grandmother.

Anne related her story in a lengthy interview with Susan Hadler:

My mother said that on the morning my father died, she was dusting the house and that she saw him in front of her. She said it was very strange because she had never seen him in battle dress before. He appeared before her in the dining room and she saw him in a helmet and khakis. She thinks he came to say goodbye.

I grew up with my mother in my grandmother's house and was extremely close to both of them. My mother loved my dad. A lot of that love rubbed off on me. I was close to her family, and there were a lot of other grandchildren.

When I was around eleven or twelve, I discovered my father's letters hidden away in my mother's dresser. While she was out, I used to read them in secret. It was wonderful because he had been very excited about my birth. He would send letters in blue envelopes and then next in pink envelopes. He was very happy about having a baby. He called me the papoose! It made me feel like I was a part of them, together.

He also talked a lot about why he felt he wanted to be in the infantry and why it was the right thing for him to do. You could feel the absolute commitment and belief that he had in what he was doing. That makes it better for me. The heartbreak is, of course, that he died so close to the end of the war. That drives me crazy.

Some of the men he [served] with came to visit Mom over the years. They used to just drop in. They made Mom laugh. They would show up in her office, come in, sit down, and say, "I just came to see how you were doing and what was going on." It was really nice and very good for her. The first time I was married one of them, who had named his daughter after me, sent me a wedding present. He had come to our house numerous times. He was very tall, a big man like my dad. He always used to sit in the smallest chair we had, and my mother would say, "Oh, my God! That chair is going to fall apart!"

Recently Anne was given a letter from her father's war buddy, Alfred. The letter had been written on May 24, 1945, to Al's sister who had asked what he would like for his birthday. As his present, Al asked his sister to visit Ed's family. He begins with an explanation about their wartime friendship:

It was early March when Ed first joined our outfit—he came in as a replacement from the States. He was a sergeant and had been in the army four years as an M.P. He was thirty-four years old. His home is in Englewood, N. J. He came into our outfit and was a rifleman in my squad. Fortunately when he joined us the breakthrough of the Siegfried line was in effect and there was very little fighting for us. He hadn't been in any fight at all. We went back to a rest area for a week and then moved to an engineer unit to help work on a road across the Rhine—still no action.

Finally we got our orders. We were crossing the Rhine and going to continue moving ahead. The movements consisted mostly of short motor rides, hikes, and cleaning out towns. There was very little fighting. We kept on the move continuously for about two weeks then we came upon the Weser River. We stayed in a town for two days and then we were told we would move across the river.

It was around April 5th that we crossed a river and moved toward a town. It was here that Ed saw his first action, for we had received heavy fire from German artillery and mortars. It was here also that our platoon caught a lot of trouble. Joe, my assistant squad leader, had to take prisoners back and I was very busy—so I put Ed in charge of some men—he did a magnificent job and showed that he was cool under fire. I knew then he was a good man.

The following morning we moved out and attacked the city of Hann-Münden. It was here that Joe was hit by a sniper bullet and had to be evacuated. Ed became my assistant squad leader. It was here too, that I received my small wound in the hand. It didn't amount to anything, but several days later it started to get infected. So I had to have it treated by the medics. The only thing I could do was soak my hand in hot water and salt. During this time we joined the Combat Command A and started driving toward Leipzig.

We rode all day on tanks and trucks, and I didn't have time to soak my hand. We would stay in a town at night [and] it was then that I had my only opportunity to soak my hand. Everyone would sleep, and I had to sit up and soak my hand for an hour or so. But there was one guy that stayed with me—Ed Moloney. He would keep the water hot and see that I kept soaking it.

It was during one of these sessions that Ed and I had a long talk. We stayed up to 2 A.M. and while I soaked my hand we talked and talked. He talked mostly about his wife and the baby she was expecting. He always said it's going to be a boy and his name is going to be Edwin, Jr. He said, "you know, Al, when my wife and I got married we decided we'd have to work fast for we are both getting older." Then he said, "I sort of surprised myself hitting the jackpot!" Ed was really quite a humorist and he'd tell a joke and keep a straight face. He never changed his tone of voice whether he was mad, or kidding at any time. Many a time when we got to a town and had champagne we would toast to Ed, Jr.

It was at six o'clock on the 13th of April that we got orders to move out and set up a road block that the Germans were retreating on. Our company moved out that night and we had five tanks in support. It was dark when we got to our position so we went ahead and dug in. I went on a patrol that night and found there was a German ack-ack [anti-aircraft] position about 500 yards away. I was given the assignment to knock the position out. I was to leave with a fifteen-man patrol at dawn to move in on their position.

I had men from all three squads, and we moved toward the German position. (We were told previously by a Frenchman there were only six men there.) We were fired on by a few rifles but we kept going. Suddenly about fifty Germans got up and ran—so we took out after them. It was then that they fired on us with time fire (shells bursting in air over our heads). The patrol reached a dugout and we were safe, but we couldn't move, for the minute we'd show ourselves, they would open fire with artillery. We were trapped out there, and I called on the radio for the tanks to help us out. I couldn't get the radio working and I had to send back a messenger. In about half an hour the tanks came with infantry behind them. They really raised hell with the Germans and drove them out of their position. At the same time the Germans started laying down a terrific barrage of overhead fire and the men were helpless. (Moloney had come out with the rest of the squad with the tanks.) We received the order to pull back and that was the last time I saw Moloney alive—I was just getting ready to leave with the radio when he passed by and I waved to him.

Our casualties were very high, and I immediately went to company to put in a call for more medics. I was gone for 20 minutes and when I returned someone said that everyone was told I was killed. Our Lieutenant said he gave me last rites out there. Everyone had mistaken Moloney for me. For we did resemble each other. Believe me I felt mighty funny when one fellow told me he saw *me* lying out there. A fellow that saw Moloney said it was very fast, for he was killed instantly. I have been praying that Ed's wife had the baby before she received word of the death of her husband.

Possibly you have guessed what I have in mind. When I come home I am going to visit Ed and I want you to pay his wife and child a visit some Sunday that you have time. It's a different job for you but it would please me a great deal.

I don't know whether the baby is a boy or girl. So I would appreciate it if you would do this favor for me. I am going to write his wife as soon as this letter is on its way in about a week. I won't mention your visit though in case you don't want to go. Love to all. Your loving brother, Alfred

Anne continued her recollection as a war orphan in her conversation with Susan:

I feel fortunate that I was very close to my father's family. There was an important connection through them. I knew what his family was all about. I think I idealized them but that was okay because that got me through some perils as well.

I went through a phase of thinking I was really illegitimate and they never were going to tell me. But that didn't last because here was Uncle Frank and Aunt Evelyn! Here were the pictures. I had one aunt who I used to spend a lot of time with and who, when all her kids were asleep, would sit at the kitchen table with me and say, "Well now, has your mother told you about your father?" I would say no, and she would tell me things about him. I don't remember what she told me now. But she was the only person who ever talked about him to me.

I was very lucky to know a lot of his friends. He was a big basketball star at his high school, and I used to go and present a big trophy in his name each year. A lot of people who knew him would see me and say, "Oh, she looks just like Ed." I did have a sense of him, but it was never enough.

From time to time my mother would tell me, "Oh, you're just like your father," or "You sleep with your knees up just like your father did." I would hang on to these words. But I would never have the nerve to ask anything else. When you are a very small child, you learn there are things you should not ask. I believe there was so much pain that my mother never shared or expressed. What she says is, "If I started to cry, I would never stop." I think that to be pregnant, to have your husband die, to be scared to death with how are you going to bring up your child, and how are you going to have enough money is very traumatic, beyond words. And on top of all this, the war ends, and everybody comes home and seems happy. I think it was terrible and it was a time when people didn't sit down easily with someone who could help them through tough times. I don't think she ever talked about it. I think she just shut the door.

My mother lost everything she was waiting and hoping for. It wasn't as if she had it and lost it. It was what she was waiting for. She only dreamed of having it. There were an awful lot of perfect linen tablecloths that never got used. So many things that were being saved for a time in the future that never happened.

Recently I got up the courage to ask my mother about her wedding. She said, "Well, we got married at a mass in the church, and the couple that got married just before us, had the same luck. He was killed, too. The same thing happened to us. There was never enough time, never enough." It was very hard for me to ask those questions.

My mother worked very hard and put me through very good schools. She is now eighty-four years old and still working. I kid her sometimes and say she had better stay in shape because when she dies she's going to be married to a much younger man. She is still very attached to my father's memory and has dreams about him from time to time.

My mother and I are extremely close. We are a team. A couple of years ago she was ill, and I really thought she might not recover. The feeling I had at that time was that it had always been the two of us against the world. That didn't even bring in my grandmother whom we lived with and whom I adored. There was just the two of us that had to survive. She did everything she possibly could to make my life a good one, and nobody would understand how it was just two of us and what that meant or how strong that bond is.

There was so much about him that was unspoken. That is a difficult thing for us. We talked a little bit but it was scary at times. I don't know what's so scary. I've talked about many things that were much worse in my life. I don't know what is so taboo. The questions I have are really about the other half of me and how that comes together. Who I am.

I never, never talked about it with friends at school either, because everybody else had fathers. I was the only one. That is how I felt. That I was so different and I was ashamed of being different. There was a feeling of being insecure and different. Kids go through this phase where they want to be alike, wear the same thing, have the same haircut. So it didn't make me feel good to be different. I remember being in the third grade. Somebody else's father died. I was so excited. I fell in love immediately with the boy whose dad died.

When I was twenty-four years old and working in New York, I met another girl whose father had been killed at Pearl Harbor. We were friends for a long time. We used to talk about our dads dying. She was four or five, so she remembered her dad; she had the experience of losing a dad she knew. She shared it with me. She had a sense of isolation about that and about her experiences which were there in her first marriage, and they were there in my first marriage. We felt outside of the marriage. Outside the relationship, in a way. I think it was that kind of thing: "I will go it alone." That fear of abandonment and that you better just do it yourself.

I have worked all my life and have been fairly successful. A great deal of that comes from believing you can't rely on anybody because they will go away. You have got to make sure that, unlike your mother, who was working for $25.00 a week and hoping to make it all stick together, you can take care of yourself. I am only now beginning to let go some of that, and it is a positive thing. I don't want to let it go too far, but it is nice not to feel something will come out of nowhere and you will be stranded. It is too scary relying on somebody else.

I have always felt that I was born in the wake of death and it has shed its pale on my life. I don't know how to explain that. My life has been a very good one. I have a wonderful mother. I was close to her family which had a lot of other grandchildren in it even though I was an only child. I think I had a very happy life and I've been very lucky. It is just this one thing that never went away. It is the only thing I have in life that is really hard for me.

When John F. Kennedy was assassinated, I was a freshman in college. His death really blew me away because I had idolized him and thought he was wonderful and glamorous. I think his death initiated a mourning for my dad, something that I had not done. Three years after Kennedy's death, I went to Europe where my father is buried. I left the friend I was traveling with in Paris and went by myself to the Netherlands on the train. I sat with a Belgian nun and a German businessman. We talked about what I was doing. It felt bizarre because I had grown up not having a great view of the Germans or Europe in general. Since then I have been many times and even lived there for a couple of years. I have a whole different feeling now.

The cemetery is in Margraten, Holland, and is very beautiful. I was so glad I was by myself. It was something that felt very private. It was so good to see the place, to see that he had really existed. The stone cross on his grave was a real, concrete thing, and I could say, "This is the place." It was some kind of closure and yet it was an opening. My father and I had never been in the same spot together before.

Every time I go to visit my father's grave, I bury a quarter down in the ground because it's something I touched. I always make sure I have an American quarter with me when I visit.

Several years after my first visit, I took my mother. It was wonderful. Apparently many years before she had asked a friend to locate the cemetery and his grave but they couldn't find it. So she never asked again. I found it easy enough. It is a great big beautiful cemetery. It was really, really important that I take her there. She was extremely proud. The American who is there running the place said, "Would you like to have your photograph taken?" Mom said, "Yes, I would." So she stood there so proudly next to the cross and had her photograph taken. It was like the last photograph that my parents had taken standing together at a bus stop when he was leaving to go into New York to leave on the ship. Standing there so proudly beside his cross, she looked the same way she looked in that earlier picture, except that she was twenty-two years older. I was deeply moved. It was a wonderful thing that she now knew where he was.

I always regret that my father was buried overseas. You need to know where a person is. If you are a child and you don't know where your father is, then he could be walking around anywhere. As a child, I always used to have this image that my dad would just come walking up the street and that he would have been a prisoner of war, gotten lost, or something.

For me I think anything that was physical was important. I didn't have anything else. It was that great desire to touch something. I think my mom was the same way. I had an old cigar box. She had my dad's handkerchiefs. They were all monogrammed. She gave them to Steven, my husband, as a Christmas present last year. I said to him later: "That's all that is left of my dad, and when she gave them to you it was a really significant gesture." He is very sympathetic. He is Jewish and he identifies a lot with the war. But for him that whole war was a very terrible thing. We both enjoy studying the history of World War II. We read together. When we go to the cemetery, as we did three or four times when we lived in England, he has a compassion that maybe not everybody would have. I will talk about it, and he will say at least it was a good cause and he feels strongly about that. That makes me feel better.

I find myself a little nuts about my own death. What drives me nuts about it is not *dying*; it is not *being there*. I am beginning to try to talk about this. I think there is a connection between the fear of dying and the fear of not being there. It is not that I will be in such great pain or anything. It's not being there. Whatever that is relates to my dad not being there. I used to think I would never live beyond thirty-five years old, the age my father was when he died. I thought, "Coming up on thirty-five, better watch out."

Also as a child I developed a strong level of intuition about what is going on with other people. There is also a need that I have to fix things for everybody else. If somebody else is sad or not happy, I have to fix it. I think I need to fix it. I think there is a connection with taking things in without ever talking about all those feelings. I always have a sense of what is going on, what people are feeling, and I act in a very intuitive way. It doesn't often lead me that far astray. It must come from being tuned in at an early age.

I identify with President Bill Clinton in a way because his father died before he was born. There are things that he says sometimes that I understand. His need to say, "We'll make it feel better." And the way he needs to always please everybody so that everything is okay. I read a quote that he was really too soft inside. It may appear that way but I would suspect it is not true. We may be soft, but inside there is an incredible ability to know exactly what it is you have to deal with to survive and what your strengths are. So while he appears to be appeasing all factions I don't believe it is true.

My first marriage was to a man I thought I could fix. One of those situations where you fall in love with somebody and it's great and you're very happy but there are significant problems and you think you will teach him what a happy family is all about. That whole feeling of, "I'll fix it. I'll make it all okay." And the fact is you can't always do that. I couldn't. The best thing I learned was that I couldn't fix other people's problems. They have to fix them.

I think I missed out on learning about relating to men. For me it was a double whammy because I only went to girls' schools my whole life. That wasn't the greatest idea. I had to be thirty years old before I had an easiness with men or men who were friends without putting them on a pedestal. I always had this ideal about what it was supposed to be like with men. Real life is never like that. Also the fear of abandonment was a big deal. I always had a fear he would go away. I still worry about my husband when he goes out to walk the dog and it seems to be taking a little longer. I think, "Oh, my God, he got shot on the street, or something." I get crazy. I have to just chill out. I keep thinking he's going to be taken away.

I think my mother still feels like something bad is going to happen, that something's going to be taken away. Yet from the moment my dad died nothing ever changed in her life. She never remarried. She never had more children. She lived in the same house for years and years. Nothing ever really changed. Now she's eighty-four years old and she still goes to work four days a week. She has tremendous spunk and she's very bright and has lots of interests. She always has seen herself as apart, too, as separate. She is really a remarkable person and is very active, but there is always that separateness. That is something I have, too.

I do feel that when my mother dies, she will be with him, that it will be a good thing, and when I die, I will be with both of them. That will be a good thing. It's not that he's floating up in the sky, but I think that there is a presence. I don't know what it is. He's sort of always with me. I used to feel I was never alone because he was always there.

What I think about now is, "How in God's name am I ever going to make this okay?" I have a very happy marriage. I don't have any children but I have inherited three who are terrific. My mother and I have come through whatever battles we had along the way. You get to this point of rest and you think, "Well, I better figure out now what the second half of my life is." But I don't know how, in God's name, I'm ever going to feel okay about my father's death and absence from my life. It's just the one thing that never goes away. I can be trucking along through my life and something can happen and I feel like I'm sideswiped by tears.

I would like to be at peace. I don't mean that it would go away but that I would feel better about myself. I don't know where that place is. I don't know why it's hard to figure out. I know as much as I am probably going to know so it is not more information that I need. I can talk about just about anything, but it's funny, if we go someplace and the subject comes up about dying or the war, Steven will say, "Well, Anne has a special interest." Then I feel like OH MY GOD. Sometimes I say something, sometimes I don't. I can be so thunderstruck by that recognition. Why isn't it natural to talk about it? Nobody did, and that is why I can't and that is why I don't.

I have a very good friend whose father died when she was five. I was with her, her mother, and her sister for dinner. The mother constantly talks, "Remember when your daddy took you to the pool?" or "Remember when daddy this and that?" It was a whole night of remembering. I said to her later, "I find it astounding that even though you feel badly about your father's dying, your mother talks about him as if he's there, he's with you." My mother never said, "Daddy and I couldn't wait for you to be born," or "Daddy and I would have wished." I never had that.

When I read an article in the *Washington Post* about a ceremony for World War II war orphans in Washington, D.C., I sat at the breakfast table, with the dog hopping around, and I was crying my eyes out reading this article. Because the article talked about people not talking!

We war orphans are all getting to be fifty and we're just dealing with this and remembering. I find myself wanting to immerse myself in it. I feel like what I want to do for my fiftieth birthday is go back to Europe and take the same path that my dad took. I was talking to Steven about it and he said, "Oh, well, I'm sure everything has changed." That is exactly what I need to do. That is exactly what I want to do. I just want to go.[1]

[1]Interview with Susan Hadler on October 5, 1993; additional material on September 9, 1996; letter of Alfred to Charlotte, May 24, 1945; all material in AWON files.

Ceal and Ed Moloney, 4 February 1945 at Ceal's home in Englewood, New Jersey. "Last visit home for Ed Moloney."

*Anne Moloney, October 1947,
Englewood, New Jersey.*

Anne Moloney Black visiting her father's grave at Margraten, Netherlands, Winter 1968.

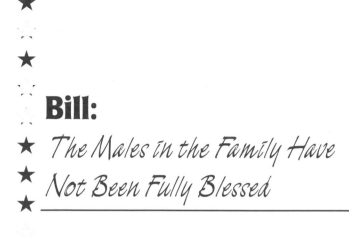

Bill:

The Males in the Family Have Not Been Fully Blessed

*W*orld War II took almost all of the adult males in Bill's family. His father, Thompson Brook Maury, III; his grandfather on his mother's side, Paul Belmont Bunker; and a grand-uncle, Weymin Beehler, were all West Point graduates and all served in the war. None of them survived. Another uncle died in a bomber crash prior to Pearl Harbor. Only an uncle who served in the Corps of Engineers came back from the conflict.

Bill was born in November 1939, at Ft. Lewis, Washington, where his father was then stationed in the field artillery. His grandfather served in the coast artillery. At the time of Pearl Harbor, the Army had ordered both officers to the Philippines, where they would later die as POWs.

After his father left for the Far East in June 1941, Bill, his mother, and his older brother and sister moved to Los Angeles, along with a younger sister, born two days before Bill's father had shipped out. They were joined in the household by his maternal grandmother, whose husband was then serving on Corregidor, by Aunt Betsy, whose husband had died in a prewar bomber crash, and by Aunt Betsy's daughter.

Prior to his father's death, Bill remembers his wartime childhood in a house full of women as a happy one. Despite the fact that his father, his grandfather, and his grandmother's brother were all away fighting the war, the household was not gloomy:

It wasn't a sad household, remarkably. There was a lot of stuff going on, but what did I know? As a little kid I viewed it as happy. A lot of women were around there. It seemed very happy. My mother was working at Lockheed as a spot welder, and then she was always very good at drafting and became a tool designer. We weren't hurting for money. We were getting money from my father who was at that time a major and my grandfather who was a full colonel.

Bill's grandfather died in a Japanese prison camp on May 8, 1943, which was the day of his grandfather's birthday, and one year after the surrender of Corregidor. Though a young child, Bill remembers his grandmother's reaction:

My grandmother was a very interesting woman, very, very bright and very capable in a lot of ways. She had joined the WACs, but she was a very heavy drinker. I don't remember much about it, except that occasionally she would be sort of *hors de combat,* and she wouldn't be around. I remember her falling down a couple of times. She lived with us until she died in 1961, and she didn't drink at all in later years, didn't have any drinks in the house.

Bill's father died in 1944. The news that he was missing and presumed dead arrived just before Christmas.

We were all called into my mother's room. By that time Aunt Betsy had left with her daughter and gone back east. Mom had a big bed, and she got us all up on it and said, "Your father's dead." That was the end of that, and she quit working in the war effort right then, because the war was just about over. So it was a grim time. But she was a tough cookie in a lot of ways.

The circumstances of his father's death were particularly tragic. As the war turned and the United States took the offensive, the Japanese packed American prisoners into Japanese merchant ships for transit to Japan. American bombers and submarines, without knowing that the ships contained their countrymen, sank many of these infamous "hell ships" before they reached Japan:

In 1944 the Japanese were increasingly coming on hard times, and they didn't want to put up with these prisoners they had caught. So they took my father and his prison camp and stuck them on their troop ships. They were anchored in the middle of Manila Bay. All the hatches were nailed down. There was no way for the men to get out. They were simply—they were like people who were buried in sand, they simply couldn't escape. A number of them died from the heat before they were bombed. There was terrible heat below. It was as hot as the hinges of hell.

My father was in charge of a group and, according to people— some survived—he was constantly trying to figure out ways to get air to circulate, because the heat was overwhelming, and many of the prisoners were sick anyhow. It was like a slave ship. American airplanes spotted and bombed the ships. There was no marking that these were POW ships. The bombers thought they were Japanese troop ships, because they were all marked with Japanese insignia and stuff. It was a terrible thing for the Japanese to do, absolutely miserable.

Bill's family remained in Los Angeles until 1947, when they moved to the Washington, D. C. area, living first in Rockcrest, Maryland, and later settling in Garrett Park, in the same state. Tragedy continued to follow the family, however, as polio struck Bill's sister and juvenile diabetes hit his older brother. In addition, Bill's remaining grandfather died, removing an important link to his father.

Once his son was killed, he just sort of gave up the ghost. He died. My father's father. He had been a very active and busy newspaper man but when his son died he just sort of cashed it in. He wasn't very old. I guess he died when he was about sixty. But he just said to heck with it. It was not worth it for him. He gave it up. My father was his only child. I don't remember much about him.

As with many orphans, Bill felt the childhood shame and burden of being without a father.

One of the things that I had, that all of us had, I think, was sort of shame that our parents were killed in the war. It was very remarkable, but the first thing my mother said when my father died was that we shouldn't tell anybody. We shouldn't be in a position that we were victims. Don't make yourself into a victim.

I remember very well having a Boy Scout meeting or something like that, and everybody was supposed to bring his father, and I just felt really terrible about it, that I didn't have a father to bring. I must have been eleven or twelve, something like that. But thinking that anybody [would have been okay], even some old stumble-bum off the street, just somebody there, if I just had somebody there to stand up and talk about. Then at an awards banquet in sports, too, I would always have to have somebody else's father stand up.

I had, that I'm aware of, one sort of acquaintance in high school whose father was killed. Her name was Paula. Her father was killed at Iwo Jima. She had a brother named Paul. And they were similar to us in a lot of ways. The mother was a school teacher and was doing everything on her own. Paula was very pretty—not real smart, but very creative. Paul was sort of a hell-raiser. Both of them became very dysfunctional. Paula eventually committed suicide. I don't even know what happened to Paul.

Additionally, Bill felt that he never knew his father as a person. There was no connection to a real human being. Instead, there was only a single photograph, an icon on a wall.

As far as my mother was concerned, my father was raised up in front of us kids as this paragon, this thing that could not possibly be matched in anything. My father was very handsome. I don't look very much like him. My brother looks almost exactly like him, and my nephew, who committed suicide, looked almost exactly like him. I look like my grandfather, the one who died on Corregidor, and I was always a favorite of my grandmother. She thought I was the cat's meow. I felt that I was very much loved as I was growing up. But I also felt that the idea of my father was something that I could not possibly attain. The idea that he would do anything wrong was just beyond anything. I didn't think of him per se, of taking a leak or something. He was beyond that. I never had a chance to face the old wolf ever in my life. . . .

My father's name came up very seldom in the house. . . . I never had any sense that he existed. There's one picture. There was no connection to his life. . . . I don't have any stories about him as a kid. I don't have any idea how he was as a child, if he ever did anything wrong, if he ever got drunk or screwed somebody when he was fifteen. I have no idea. I have no connection with that. All of the connections I had that came back were filtered through a woman's eyes, whether it was his mother or my mother. It never dawned on me until this very moment—I don't know anything at all about him, nothing, nothing at all.

I remember when I got into West Point, I think it was the only time that my father's name was brought up. My mother said, "I know your father would be very pleased, very proud of you." My mother, I don't know if she was proud. She didn't say that she was proud. She said my father would have been very proud.

Going to West Point seemed both natural and inevitable to Bill. After all, there was the military tradition of the family.

We've been around for years and years and years, mostly southern, which of course is a different—really, at that time, was a different country. There was a very strong, very enduring military tradition that went with it. We believed very firmly in the government, the army, in the military, whether it was the navy or the army, and we continued to support it and did what we were told to do.

My brother, who had diabetes, couldn't go to West Point and my cousin Paul, who was somewhat of a dim bulb anyhow, also got married when he was seventeen and obviously couldn't go to West Point. So the one person left to carry on the tradition of the thing was me.

Additionally, the war added its own impact.

I always thought I was going to die young, because all the people had died young. It seemed to me that my path was pretty well laid out that I was going to West Point and then die young. It just seemed preordained. That's the way it would go. . . . It was like this was some sort of grail that I had to follow, and finally capture. And when I got to West Point, I hated it. I despised it. It wasn't me. It wasn't what I wanted to do.

Bill spent three years at West Point before flunking out. His time at the Academy forced Bill to consider the cost of war to his family:

I didn't think of all the people in my family who had died particularly—I only thought of my father—until I was quite a bit older. I mean, I guess it was sort of squashed down or tamped down or what-have-you. I just didn't think that much about it. When I was at West Point, I began to have pretty grave reservations about what the purpose of my existence was—to kill or be killed. I didn't like that, and I remember having a sort of apotheosis one time when I was sitting there in class. . . . We were talking about the development of tactical nuclear weapons, and there was a discussion going on. It was a large group of people sitting in one of those amphitheaters. A colonel was talking, and he was saying, sort of offhandedly, like it didn't have that much effect, if you push a button, you can obliterate a division [15,000 men]. Jesus Christ, man, we're talking about thousands of people. You're not talking about a division. You're talking about people. And I increasingly thought, "This is not my cup of tea."

Bill finished his undergraduate work at the University of Maryland and then completed a Ph.D. in history at George Washington University. He worked for a time as an historian but then left the profession. He then drifted into computer work. Currently, he works for a newspaper. He has been married and divorced twice. Alcohol abuse has made the situation more difficult.

Looking back, he has tried to analyze the effects of his family's multiple war deaths on himself, his mother and his brother.

It didn't dawn on me until really quite recently the horror that my mother went through. My mother simply suppressed it. She was a very happy person generally, although she was incredibly moody really. She was incredibly self-centered, she and all of us kids really are, but the person who takes after her the most is my brother. He's the Sun King as far as everything is concerned, and he cannot understand anything that doesn't specifically revolve around him. But in my mother's case the understanding of how it came about is not that hard to see because everything just began to fall apart. External forces started to impinge on her from everywhere—her father, her brother, her father-in-law, her husband, uncle, all these people getting killed and just falling like flies. So it was a devastating thing for her. She continued to sort of push on, but really didn't have any particular faith that hard work or anything would get her anywhere.

What happened is our family had no males. All of that generation and the previous generation had been killed off except for one uncle. So there were no males around, and I think it had a pretty strong effect on us. . . . The views that my brother and I gathered were all female views. I mean, those were the views that we gathered. We didn't gather views that were male.

Then, in addition to that, I was very used to having women tell me what to do. It was a matriarchal society.

So I think that was very difficult for me, and it was very difficult for my brother, too. Both of us had horrendous times dealing with men. I think a lot of it probably had an effect as far as our drinking was concerned, because once you drink, then everybody's pretty much equal and everybody's laughing and having a good time and you're not weighing anything in particular. So that had a long effect on that. Of course, it was worse on my brother because he had diabetes, and he shouldn't have been drinking at all. But he drank an awful lot.

I had real difficulties in getting along with a male. I had difficulty making eye contact with them. Women professors thought I was sliced bread, but male professors, it was terrible. It was really horrible.

It is very complex, but I'm quite sure that a lot of it has to do with never having any kind of situation of dealing with a male, never having any kind of thing of being able to talk with one.

I don't think that either my brother or I expected to live very long. I think that's one of the reasons my brother became such a horrendous alcoholic and such a wild person. I was a heavy drinker and certainly didn't fulfill any kind of promise and was very lacking in a lot of things, but I wasn't as wild as he was.

Having grown up in a family without males, Bill sees an analogy between his family and many fatherless contemporary African-American families in the inner cities.

Christ, this thing can't solve itself in a generation because I'm not solved in a generation. This thing is going to go on and on and on and on, and something has got to be done.

The guy there, there he is and then his life is snuffed out, and then there is this long trail of stuff. I mean, I even look at my son, and I think, "Jesus, the effect is reaching to him." He was a very—it's very difficult. Because of my role as a father and that extends to the relationship I had with his mother, he's had a troubled youth. . . . And my brother's son is not doing too well. The males in the family have not been fully blessed.[1]

[1]Interview with Susan Hadler, December 1993; AWON files.

The Maury family in L.A. in the summer of 1944. L-R: Anne, Sally, Priscilla (mother), Richard, and Bill.

Joyce:
You Need to Talk to Your Daddy about Certain Things

*J*oyce never knew her father. Born and raised in Collinsville, Alabama, she was three months old and her sister two years old when the news arrived that their father, Wilbur Nelson Freeman, was dead. Wilbur served in Company K, 405th Infantry Regiment, 102nd Division, and died on February 16, 1945. At the time, her father's division was operating along the Roer River in western Germany in preparation for crossing that river, an assault which came one week later. Joyce does not know either the circumstances of his death or exactly where he died.

When I was a kid in school I got made fun of, laughed at, everything like that because I didn't have a daddy. But I overcome it. I went on to finish my school. My mamma never did remarry. I lived with my mamma until I got to twenty-two years old and got married. I have two boys, one twenty-six and one twenty-four. I've been divorced since I was twenty-nine years old.

Mamma never did talk about Daddy too much. It was somethin' she never did talk about. It was somethin' she said was too painful and she never would talk about him. I didn't understand it at the

31

time and feel it would have been better if we talked but she never would. She still won't. She's in a nursing home now. I used to get aggravated at her because she wouldn't talk about it. But she gets aggravated at me because she thinks I want to talk about it too much. Almost everybody thinks that. They say I'm hooked on World War II. But I talk about it anyhow. I talk to a neighbor a lot who was in the Philippines. He likes to talk about the war. I've talked to other people around home.

Our town used to be pretty big, but after the war it started goin' downhill. They are trying to get it built back up but I'll believe it when it happens. We used to have a picture show when we was kids, but they closed that up. We have a Baptist church. And we have a "caring place" down here in Collinsville that's run by the church and they give to people that needs clothes and stuff like that. We have that. We don't even have a doctor or a drug store here right now. It's sad, but that is just the way it is.

Mamma never did ask nothin' much from the government. When we were kids we never did get everything we had comin' to us because Mamma didn't ask for it. We got cheated out of a lot of stuff we were entitled to because Mamma didn't know how to ask. I just found that all out a couple of years ago. Mamma didn't know.

Daddy's buried in a cemetery out here on Sand Mountain. Near Fyffe, Alabama. . . . I went to the train station when they brought Daddy back. I remember telling everyone that was my daddy in the coffin. I was little but I remember that.

I don't work no more now. I used to but now I have bad hearing problems and some other disabilities so now I just stay home and try to do the best I can. I used to work in chicken houses and stay with elder people and help them. Mostly I had to take care of my son. He has been sick and disabled most all his life. He was born mentally retarded, but you can't tell it now. He's outgrown it pretty good. He's had a lot of surgeries and he's got eye troubles. He still lives with me. I've had it pretty rough but I guess I haven't had it any rougher than anybody else. I try to do the best I can. It gets complicated sometimes, and boy I get upset sometimes and I let off a little steam. Sometimes I get out and take a broom and work on a tree. It helps me, to let off steam.

I ain't got no pictures of my daddy. All I've got is a picture of his outfit he was in. My sister's got some pictures. But we didn't have many pictures of Daddy. Mamma said he was a good person. Everybody tells me that Wilbur was a real nice, good, kind, sweet person. He liked to aggravate you if he could aggravate, they said. He'd get ya. He liked to tease. The more he'd make you mad the worser he'd do it. That's what all my aunts and uncles told me.

I never did go around my daddy's family too much. They tried to keep us from drawing offa Daddy [collecting benefits] when Daddy got killed overseas in the Second War. They lied and everything else to try to keep us from drawing offa Daddy. They wanted to draw it themselves. We didn't draw for a good while. That's what Mamma told me and then I recently got Daddy's VA file and it was in there. But they went and told that Mamma and Daddy was divorced and all that stuff and got it all messed up. We liked to never got it. But we finally got benefits. But that made me feel ashamed, just kinda bad. I never see 'em too much. Just every once in awhile. Most of 'ems dead now.

My daddy had everything made to Mamma. And they was married. They [his family] tried to say they wasn't married, but they was. Mamma had a marriage certificate and she got Granddaddy and Grandma to fill out affidavits that they was married. Grandma and Grandpa helped take care of all of us until Mamma started gettin' her benefits. We lived with them for a good while. They lived out at Dawson, near Sand Mountain. They was awful good to us.

Sometimes when you need somebody to talk to and don't have nobody to talk to, you need to talk to your daddy about certain things. It's just hard certain days. You think he oughta be here with you but he's not. There's certain days I'll be sittin' here and I think his spirit is right here in the room with me. It's probably not so, but that's how I feel. And I've had dreams about him. People think that's odd because I never did see him, but there's times I've had dreams about him and I don't guess it's something unusual. There are times when

I wonder why he got killed. Why the Germans wanted to kill him. But that was just war and something that happened. Sometimes it bothers me. I used to hold it against the Germans. But I don't no more. I enjoyed all that Normandy Day celebration. I watched it and I watch a lot of these specials on TV tryin' to find out somethin' about Daddy.[1]

[1]Interview with Ann Mix, April 1994, and February 1997; AWON files.

Wilbur Nelson Freeman, back row, left, at mess house circa 1945.

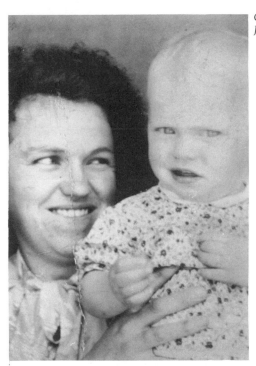

Conola Freeman and her daughter Joyce in 1946.

Conola Freeman and her daughters Melba (left) and Joyce (right), after the burial of Wilbur Nelson Freeman, February 1949, in DeKalb County, Alabama.

Wilbur Nelson Freeman's funeral, February 1949.

Honor guards salute Wilbur Nelson Freeman, February 1949.

Eric:
I Don't Think You Ever Get over It

$\mathcal{S}$amuel "Sonny" Rosen enlisted in the Naval Reserves in 1936 at the age of twenty-seven. At the time, he worked in the family business to help support his younger brothers and sisters. In 1940, as war edged closer to the United States, the government called him to active duty. His last assignment was on the USS *Spence*, a 2100-ton *Fletcher* class destroyer with the Pacific Fleet. In December 1944, the *Spence* served as part of Admiral Forrest Sherman's Task Group 38.3, operating off Luzon in the Philippines. On the 18th, a devastating typhoon struck the ships. The *Spence*, running light because of a low fuel level and continuously hammered by the storm, staggered and shuddered, then rolled heavily to port and disappeared under the waves. One officer and twenty-three enlisted men survived. Sonny Rosen was not one of them.[1]

Sonny had married in September 1944, while on leave. He and his new bride Ethel had spent seventeen days together as husband and wife before he had returned to his ship. Their son, Allen Eric Rosen, was born in June 1945.

Although Sonny and Ethel had known each other for many years, relations between the two families never were good. That complicated and flawed relationship was unchanging and left a deep mark on young Eric.

I can describe the relationship. My mother's mother's sister's brother married my father's mother. So they had a common uncle. I think cousins of cousins. But there was serious bad blood between the families. My father's family lived in a tenement in Roxbury, Massachusetts. My father was the oldest of three boys. When he was about four or five years old his youngest brother, who was one year old, inadvertently ingested some radiator fluid. My uncle was rushed to the hospital, and it was touch and go whether or not he would live.

When my grandfather came home, he asked my grandmother what happened. She said, "Well, I stuck my head out of the window to talk to one of the neighbors." In his old-world way my grandfather said, "Well, I hope you never speak again." And she never did speak to him again. She just clammed up. She was institutionalized briefly. Then she ended up being institutionalized for almost the last seven or eight years of her life. Her diagnosis was schizophrenia. . . . She did talk to other people. But because she was very slight [and] she didn't speak much English [she had been born in Russia], the diagnosis was schizophrenia. Her last five or six years were terrible, and they say she eventually died of tuberculosis. . . . This being my mother's mother's sister, being married to this woman's brother, they all blamed my grandfather for putting her in the institution. And he got married to someone—he had a child conceived—before my grandmother died. And that's still sort of a major thing known within the family. So there was bad blood going back to this period of time [1920s]. Then my parents got married, and I don't think my grandfather was too happy about their getting married.

My mother was pregnant with me when she was notified in January that my father's ship had sunk and he was presumed dead. I was born on June 13, 1945. . . . In Jewish tradition it is prohibited to name someone after the living. The idea is to name someone after the dead so they will carry on their name. But my grandfather, because my father's body was not recovered, would not permit my mother to name me after my father in the hopes that he was still alive somewhere. And as part of the prior bad blood between the families I got named after my father's mother as my middle name. I was named after my father's mother who died in the mental institution and who my grandfather wanted no mention of her ever made. He did not want my father or his brothers to think much about her because part of it was maybe he had done her wrong. So this was kind of an "in your face" to my grandfather.

My mother and father had never lived together. . . . They were married so quickly that my father forgot to change the beneficiary on his insurance policy to my mother. His father was the named beneficiary. The payment was $10,000 which in 1945 was about the cost of a house. My grandfather kept all the money. So then all the ill feelings from my grandmother . . . came back when the man who had institutionalized her was the beneficiary of my father's insurance policy and kept the money. That was a huge source of conflict after I was born between my mother's and my father's family. We never knew what happened to the money and it was never permitted for my father's brothers to raise that issue. It was just off limits as far as he was concerned. So there was always a great deal of "bad mouthing" about my father's family by my mother's family about the institutionalization of my grandmother and then the inheritance. Although my mother didn't keep me away from my father's family, she would say, "Well, they really don't give a damn about you." Or she would add, "Do they ever come to see you? Do they call? Do they write you? No, nothing."

The families' continual animosity inflicted scars on Eric, exacerbating rather than soothing his inescapable hurt and shame over being fatherless. That crippling and perplexing feeling of shame stayed with Eric throughout his childhood.

The first memory I have of being without my father and the consequence of it was when I was in a day camp. I was about six years old. The day camp had a fair during the day, and I think I was the only child there who didn't have an adult who came to the fair. I remember one particular family and the little boy came up and said, "Where is your mother? Where is your father?" And what I told them—and I remember crying about it—is that my father had been killed in the war and my mother worked. . . . So what they did was, this family befriended me and then took me around to all the events in the fair. The boy who was there with me, we went to the same school.

I remember coming back from camp and him telling me, "Well, you owe me a lot of pennies," for his mother and father buying me whatever they were buying me. I really think at that particular point, that was like a turning point where I just said—I remember being embarrassed, crying that day, and then being further humiliated by this guy. At that point, I wasn't going to let that happen to me again. It was just something that I said I was going to do—whatever pain there was there [about my father], I was going to close it off.

I think the way I was closing that off was just not talking about my father and the loss and things like that. In school, they would ask—why they had to read your mother and father's name the first day of school every year—did they do that to you? I don't know if they do it now. But I remember a couple of times either having to say, "He's deceased," or walk up to the teacher and tell the teacher, whisper to the teacher, that he was dead.

I don't know why it was so humiliating, but shame was a real feeling at that time. That was a real feeling for me. There was a lot of shame. I just don't know why they made us feel so ashamed. My friends would never talk about the subject. It was just taboo. I think part of my mother's motivation was to protect me. So she didn't talk very much about it, and no one in the family talked very much about it, and I didn't see much of my father's family at that time. There was just that whole mystery around it. But the shame I just don't understand.

After eighth grade we went to high school where we were getting to know kids from the other schools. One of the guys said, "What does your old man do?" I couldn't answer. The other kids said, "Don't say anything; just be quiet." I was glad they said that so I didn't have to tell the new kids at the new school the story. That was when I was about thirteen.

I think a part of the shame was there were so few divorces in the fifties. You were really an anomaly if you didn't come from a two-parent home. Even adoption was kept very quiet.

Eric's relationship with his mother was complex and difficult and played a part in sending him into therapy later as an adult.

My mother told me that my father did know that she was pregnant. She had some pictures of my father. She didn't want me to feel diffcrent and suffer the pain, but she was wise enough to know it was important to have a picture around. So I had pictures. But unfortunately she tore up all his letters. A cousin did send me a photocopy of one letter they kept. So at least I had that one little letter.

My mother never said too much about my father, and what she said was often not positive. Although she said he was intelligent, she also described him as very stubborn. She would say that if he had a meal that would take an hour to eat and he only had half an hour, he would only eat half the meal. The other negative thing that she would always tell me [was] that if he had lived, I wouldn't have been as well off as I was. Basically, it was materially. We weren't, by any stretch of the imagination [rich], but in terms of my needs and wants, my mother spared nothing. She worked hard. She was a successful business woman for that era. . . . I think she wanted me to recognize all that she did, how she put herself out for me.

My mother was on the one hand very domineering and overbearing. She was tough in that respect. I don't think I was abused in the sense that they talk about it today, but I was strapped. She did hit. She had a very, very bad temper. On the other hand, she was overwhelmingly affectionate. She had really extremes of behavior.

She'd be very loving and then she could be physically and verbally abusive. She dealt with a lot of people that way. She had a very, very bad temper.

On the other hand she really killed herself [working]. . . . She wanted to be both parents. She didn't want me to feel the loss. She would constantly say, "I don't want you to be treated differently from other kids because you don't have a father." What she meant was materially. So what she did is she worked. . . . So she got to spend very little time with me and that was difficult on her and me.

I had a lot of difficulty with women because the whole center of my existence was to please women. I really grew up in a matriarchy. My mother went off to work so my mother's mother took care of me. My grandmother is the person who raised me. She was a good buffer to my mother. She was much calmer. She came from Russia. Every Friday she baked Jewish bread. It was really an old world house in a sense. We had kosher food. It was very nice in that respect. My grandmother did a good job. She was very good to me. She gave my mother someone to leave me with while she went to work. My mother paid all the bills, but at least I was able to be raised within my own family.

My mother's brother who was still unmarried at the time went to my little league games. If I was having a problem at school he would come up and see the teachers. He dealt with the situation a little better than my mother, so I had a father figure there. Even though my uncle was there as a father figure, it was clear who the boss was. He accepted it, and my mother made it clear that *she* [emphasis in the original] made the decisions that affected me. Sometimes if he crossed her there would be some very, very serious fighting in the house. It was really a matriarchy.

My mother remarried in 1961, when I was sixteen. She married a business colleague who worked for a different company. . . . I got married when I was thirty-three and most of my friends got married in their twenties. Before I got married I moved off to Washington, D.C., and went to law school there and practiced there for five years. But I ended up in therapy as a result of a relationship with a woman. . . . It became clear in therapy that I had let women pretty much run all over me largely because I was raised in a matriarchal environment and had no strong father figure. My uncle was precluded from doing that.

I never, except for one summer, lived with my stepfather. He tried really hard. He wanted me to accept him. My mother said, "You can change your name if you want." And I said, "No way. I've had this name and this is my father's name. I'm keeping that name." She said, "Well, if you were a little younger he could have adopted you." I didn't want any part of that. He tried very hard, but he was not a nice man.

He and my mother were birds of a feather. They really only had each other, and they didn't make friends because they just denigrated everybody. They were the worst gossips you can ever imagine. For the twenty-five years, from the time he and my mother got married until he died, about eight years after my mother died, they were at the heart of every family fight I can remember. They really put me in terrible positions. They caused all kinds of problems.

My mother and I had our problems, just whatever, a mother-son relationship compounded by a very strong, very domineering woman. She died in 1980.

The other side is I have difficulties in relationships with men. I had no brothers to relate to, and even though I had my uncle and my stepfather I would never let myself get completely close to men out of loyalty to my father. Even though my father was dead, and they were father figures, I would never completely open up to, or would treat, another man like a father. That caused difficulties with my stepfather in the last years of his life. And I know it has affected my relationship with my uncle. We are very close, we get along but there is that barrier—that last link that I never cross in relating to him because it would be disloyal to my own psyche. If I treat someone else like my father it is disloyal.

Eric later reestablished contact with his father's brother, the child who had drunk the radiator fluid so many years before. By then, his Uncle Barney was dying of pancreatic cancer. When his uncle first called, Eric's mother reacted with the comment: "Oh, big deal. Now you're almost thirty years old. I've educated you. I've taken care of you. What do you need them for?"

Despite his mother's remarks and the longstanding influence of her attitude toward his father's family, Eric finally responded to his uncle's initiative.

I moved back to Boston in September of '77. The day before I started work I made arrangements to go out and see my uncle. I remembered him fairly well, but he was very emaciated from chemotherapy. He said he had felt terrible about not seeing me more. He said, "I just feel really guilty. But I couldn't do it. It was too much pain for me to see you." My father was his big brother . . . and he just said he found it enormously difficult to be around me. Over the course of that year I was with him frequently, probably once a month. He wanted to talk about my father. My Uncle Barney described my father as a terrific guy, a great dancer. He told me my father was an athlete. He had to quit school to work in the family business. There was about four years difference between them, but because so much responsibility fell to my father, he seemed like he was much older. If there was a ball game, he would make sure his two brothers got in the ball game. He really took care of them. With his father working and his mother gone, he did a lot for them. And they always emphasized that he was very, very family oriented. So at least I got to know all this stuff. I'm pigeon-toed and so was he. Over the years, my mother had a few pictures that she gave me, but everybody else gave me more pictures. I [now] have a ton of all kinds of pictures of my father, when he was a teenager, at the beach, when he was in the Navy, a whole set.

I was just about the age that my father was when he died. I was in my early thirties. I looked just like him. My uncle gave me a great picture of my father, where the resemblance is striking. They would say, "You are him to us."

I was married in September of '78, a little over a year after I moved back to Boston. We were going to get married in December, but my aunt wrote and asked if we would move it up because my Uncle Barney who was dying wanted to be there. So we did and all my father's brothers and sisters were able to come. Uncle Barney died three weeks later.

In 1986, an aunt told me that they have a spot in Arlington Cemetery for people whose remains were never recovered. After about a year of correspondence we got a monument placed and the government actually ran a full naval funeral. My father's sole surviving brother and his wife, and my aunt and cousins and my wife and I flew down. The Navy had a clergyman and they had a twenty-one gun salute. They presented me with the flag. My aunt and uncle were very stoic. It was still hard. It was forty years after his death. But they were glad they were there and they were glad we did it. It was emotional for me, but there was still that shame from childhood. I don't think I cried during the funeral, but I sure did when I got home. I have the folded flag.

This psychologist that I spoke with said, at one point, there's a mourning process where the person dies and you experience grief and you can't talk about the person for a long period of time. And then you internalize your experiences with the person, and you sort of come out at the end of it. But we can never get to that step, because you can't do the experiences with your father. So I don't think you ever get over it, because there's nothing to anchor. So in that sense, I have a better sense of my father, but I don't have the sense of closure. I have more than I probably ever would have had, but it's never finished.

People who haven't been through it, don't realize it. They'll look at you and say, "Well, you had a house. You had a loving family. You got yourself educated." I used to have a doctor and I could never understand why he was saying this to me, "It's amazing you turned out so well given what you went through." He had a sense of it, but people close to it didn't have a sense of it. If you look back on it, it's incredible what you had to go through with the shame, and not mentioning it, the silence, and then having it all resonate. I feel that it was almost pulled out of me as an adult. You think, this is happening when you're forty, fifty years old. It is amazing.

I wrote to an old friend a few years ago and I was describing what I had been doing for the last fifteen or eighteen years. I really felt that the biggest achievement of my life is coming to terms with this, not through closure, . . . the funeral, getting in touch with my father's family. And she happened to understand. Others would have a hard time, I think. I think more and more people like me are getting to understand the pain of it and the loss. My wife, definitely. She encouraged me to do a lot of the therapy. I think my cousin and his wife and my uncles understand. I think they understood.

My wife wanted to get me something nice for my birthday. I had seen ads in magazines that they're remaking a lot of G.I. watches. Before we went to the store I said, "I would like something naval for my father." They actually had a remake of a watch that navy men wore and it's got the navy seal. I said to her, "I don't want you to tell anybody why I'm looking at this watch." I don't know if it's the embarrassment or the shame or what it is, but it's there. I don't drink much alcohol, but every once in a while, if I have a drink, this wells up in me. It really does.[2]

[1]For information on the *Spence,* including a photograph, see Samuel Eliot Morison, *The Liberation of the Philippines: Luzon, Mindanao, the Visayas, 1944–1945* (Boston: Little, Brown, 1969), pp. 71–87, Vol. XIII of *History of United States Naval Operations in World War II.*
[2]Interview with Susan Hadler, June 21, 1995, and Ann Mix, June 23, 1995; AWON files.

Sonny Rosen and Ethel S. Rosen, September 1944 at the Copacabana, New York, New York.

A. Eric Rosen in November, 1986, at the dedication of Rosen Square in Worcester, Massachusetts.

Connie:
I Remember the Cake . . . the Package that Came Back

$\mathcal{C}$onnie's mother Margaret was Italian, and her father, Bartolome or "Bart," was Cuban. The two sides of the family did not get along very well. Connie remembered the difficulty, commenting that "we were not that close because the Italian side didn't like the Cuban side. They looked down on the Cuban side. The Cubans looked down on the Italians because the Cubans were more educated." Bart's father was a physician who had come from Cuba to Washington's Walter Reed Hospital on a fellowship. When he returned to Cuba, Bart had remained in the capital to attend high school.

Bart had married Margaret when he was nineteen and she was eighteen. He hoped ultimately to become a translator with the Pan American Union, but first there was a wife to support. He held a variety of jobs. In 1944, he worked as a shipping clerk for a bakery. That same year, he received his induction notice. By then, he and Margaret had been married ten years and had three daughters. Margaret expected their fourth child in the fall of that year.

Bart died on February 10, 1945, in the fighting around the western German town of Schmidt. A holder of the Bronze Star, he served in Company F of the 311th Infantry Regiment, which at the time was attached to the 9th Infantry Division. His thirtieth birthday had been the previous month, and Connie recalls the birthday cake that the family had sent him that the Army then returned:

My father's birthday was January 23rd. We'd sent a birthday cake, and the cake came back before the notice of his death. My mother knew something was wrong. Now, I've gotten over it, but I never liked birthday cake. I remember the package of the cake, the brown wrapping. I can still see that to this day.

Nor was the cake the only item that came back. Connie's mother had faithfully written her husband while in the army, sending him two V-mails and two airmails every night.[1] It took awhile for the letters to arrive in Europe and be returned to the sender. By the end of the war in Europe on May 8, these letters were still reappearing. As the nation celebrated victory, Connie and her family had daily reminders of the cost of that victory.

Connie's mother had a premonition of her husband's fate:

Mother had this dream, and my father was surrounded in blood and called her name, Margaret. And she knew then something had happened, and then the cake came back. I remember she would tell us about this dream, and she was not one to have them. He was lying in a puddle of blood calling her name. Then the cake and then the telegram. I believed her and I used to think he was really calling her. I think that must have been when he died.

Connie was four years old and still remembers some of her mother's reactions and struggles to keep the family together:

I don't even remember mother crying, but I know she was in bed a lot. The priest came and said, "Oh, you should give up the children." My two older sisters were sent out to the Christ Child Home. Somehow my younger sister and I stayed with my mother. So much of it is wiped out.

Then, about the time I started kindergarten, my two sisters came back. I always remember my mother saying, "They always wanted me to give you up," and she said, "Daddy always said to keep the children no matter what."

Connie's only memory of her father was when he was home on leave prior to going to Europe:

I remember him coming up from the basement. Our cat had kittens, and I remember he went down and looked at them. And I remember him coming up in that suit [Army uniform], but that's all. That's the only visual memory that I have in my mind.

[I had a photograph.] On the back of it, he wrote, "to my darling Connie, love, Dad." But it's all gone now. That was the only handwriting that I ever had of his. I had that signed photo and I had a bunch of pictures of him from an aunt that gave me some, not when he was in the service; but I put them in storage, and when I moved, I couldn't get anybody to go get them for me, so I lost a lot of pictures that were given to me.

Circumstances sometimes forced Connie later to depend on the help of others, for polio struck her when she was in the first grade:

I was away for a year, so I didn't know all that was going on with our family. I think mother must have had some kind of a—I don't want to say breakdown, but imagine, a widow, a young mother, and all of a sudden she's got four kids and had to take care of them. My mother took in roomers. I remember we rented the upstairs.

I was in Children's Hospital in the polio ward. It was awful. You could not see your family during the quarantine. But it was not only that. We were very, very poor, so there were not a lot of toys and stuffed animals that you see these kids with in pictures in the hospitals. Poverty, even in illness, people knew about it. . . . It all sort of comes back. It was bleak.

Then coming home, I stayed home. They didn't let me go to school. I had a teacher that came to the hospital. I wanted to go to school so badly. My sisters all had gone. I had a teacher come to the house once or twice a week. Of course, they didn't take the teaching seriously. They finally put me in the health school in Washington. I was there for awhile and I fell and broke my arm.

I was in the hospital, and that was when Daddy's body came back, and I never got to go to the funeral. I don't even remember that the family talked about it.

My one sister said she just remembered all the coffins. They must have brought back a whole bunch, the ones who had been killed over there and reburied in Arlington.

I went in the sixties. Mom used to take us to Arlington. We would count ten trees up and over. We would go in the gate, and we would go there, but it wasn't tearful. It was just what you saw, those rows and rows. I was using braces and crutches, and it was hard for me to get around. But I wanted to go, but I can't remember feeling anything.

Then I remember going back after the Vietnam War and thinking: there's one grave marker, but there's a whole family under that marker, a whole family that's interred with that one person who died. It doesn't just affect the person who died.

Although without her father, Connie did have some childhood contact with adult males:

We had roomers that lived with us. They had been older, and they all had been in the war, and they [went] to Catholic University. They roomed with us. They treated me very nicely. I didn't have uncles who would come and take me places or aunts or anything like that. They would take me to the movies, and then afterwards take me for a sundae. It was wonderful. They even tutored me. I didn't get my math too good, so they had flash cards. There are little bits of good things that we would not have had. . . . I think they were more mature than the normal college age male, because they had been in a war and they were coming back to get the GI Bill.

Connie's mother rarely spoke of her dead husband, and Connie learned at an early age not to ask too many questions:

I was always very proud of my father, and I didn't know anything about [him]. I didn't know until later he had gotten the Bronze Star. My mother didn't even talk about it. Once in awhile she would say, "Well, Bart this" or "your father" that, but she didn't dwell on it. She would say, "He wanted to be a translator at the Pan American Union," because he was very good at English and Spanish and languages, but somehow he didn't get to do that. . . . I remember how important it was when I would get a little snippet from any relative about my father. I would hang on to it. . . . Of course, we were brought up that you don't ask questions. Children should be seen and not heard, and especially when you're in an Italian family if you've got any kind of defect. You're not the perfect little woman to bear children and all this kind of stuff. So you just listened. You did not say anything. It deadens that part of the brain, I think, that makes you inquisitive. . . . There was some unwritten law or unwritten rule that you didn't question.

Nor did her education at a Catholic high school help her to understand why the nation fought, what her father's role in the war had been, or the reasons leading to his sacrifice:

The war was never talked about there. I remember when we studied World War II, it was just glazed over. My God—and I was a good student—what did we miss? What the heck was I studying? We had homework and all that, but I cannot remember World War II. It was all about the Jewish people and the Holocaust, but not even that. It just wasn't there. And I'm thinking, what in the heck, did we just sleep through those years? I don't have any more textbooks from high school, but I always wanted to go back and look at some of them. Where was the war?

It was only later when Connie married that her husband, who had retired from the military, provided some background to the events of World War II.

Connie's mother never remarried. As she stated at the war's end, "I had so much love for that man. You can only get one good man, and he was good." Connie has never doubted her mother's statement, despite a later accusation from her aunt:

My aunt once said something about my father. She said that he beat my mother, and my mother never cheeped a word of this to us. I don't know if that really is true, because I think she was very jealous of the love my mother and father had, and my aunt's husband sort of left them. I don't think she really liked my father, and we were sort of looked down on, because we were Spics. So I don't really know, but my mother, I know she loved my father.

As a child, Connie had hoped that her mother would remarry. Now as she reflects on the subject, she understands why it was unlikely to happen:

My mother never remarried. I always wanted her to remarry because I wanted a stepfather. I wanted to see her happy. . . and she never did. . . . Back then, another man just did not want a woman who had four kids he would have to take care of or think he had some kind of responsibility for, because she was a package deal. That never dawned on me, and then one that had a disability, my God!

And that's another thing that people say, when they find out you don't have a father. . . . "Oh, your mother never remarried?" Right away they think that you didn't want her to remarry or something like that. That's not true.

For Connie, education represented the key to her future, a key she was determined to grasp. She would be the only one of her sisters to go to college:

I knew I had to get an education. That was my ticket out. I had to, of all the sisters, because they expected to be married. For any bit of education I got, I had to fight for it. If it were not for the GI Bill, I could not have done it. There were no family funds to send me.

I was the one who applied for the GI Bill and kept going and taking the tests. "I don't know, you're handicapped, you might not be able to do it." That's why I like tests sometimes because on that test, I could show it.

I worked all four years of college. It wasn't party time or playing. I don't ever remember going to a party during my college life. That wasn't associated with the school. I had to work. . . . I think my sisters were somewhat resentful. In fact, they say, "You're the only one in the family that ever went to college." As if it were handed to me. It was not. I had to work at everything. And it was a fight.

As an adult, Connie tutors children, which gives her additional insight into the problem of not having a father, for she has both her own experience and that of her students to consider:

I look at kids and I see when they're with their father or with their family, they just take it for granted. But then I look at the other side, too. There are so many families where there's an abusive father. You've got to think about it that way. [If you don't have a father] it's an empty, sort of an emptiness, sort of a feeling that you've been cheated a little. There's no one to take up the battle for you if you need it.

I felt the loss in high school. A lot of girls would talk about their fathers. I didn't talk about it or get sad or anything, but I knew. And I didn't start thinking it was unfair until I got out, later on, on my own and realized. You hear people say, "Oh, my parents are coming to pick us up. They're going to get me this. They're going to do this. We're going to do this together. Daddy sent me this." Then little twinges. Celebrating birthdays, yes. I didn't like to celebrate birthdays. I didn't like the cake, the round cake because that's what came back. I remember the cake. I remember the package that came back.

Connie's insights and analysis, however, cannot always lessen the pain of not having a father. The void is always there, waiting to be exposed:

I was living in Newport News, and I met one of my neighbors in the drug store and he said he was getting a birthday card for his daughter who was forty years old. And it hit me. I thought, "I will never get a birthday card from my father." And here I was, I was thirty-something. And I said, "I've never gotten a birthday card that I could read from him," and my fortieth is going to come and I'm not going to have that. And it really hit me. I remember I went home that night, and I cried and cried.[2]

[1]V-mails were written on a special form and then microfilmed by the government before being sent overseas, printed, and delivered; troops overseas also wrote V-mails back to the States.
[2]Interview with Susan Hadler, September 1993; quotes from Connie's mother come from a clipping from the *Evening Star* (Washington, D.C.), May 8, 1945; AWON files.

PFC Bartolome Castellanos, sometime between March 1944 and February 1945.

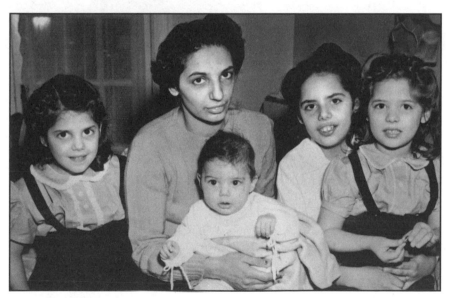

The Castellanos family in Washington, D.C., in 1945. (l-r) Mary Margaret, Mrs. Margaret Fera Castellanos (holding Barta Lea), Benita Lenora holding Connie.

Margaret F. Castellanos holding baby Barta Lea, born September 30, 1944. This photograph was sent to Bartolome.

Mary Castellanos and Connie Castellanos Caldwell at the grave of Bartolome Castellanos, Arlington National Cemetery, Memorial Day, 1992.

Damon:
They Shouldn't Send People Like That to Fight Wars

*D*amon's father, Captain George Rarey, flew P-47 Thunderbolts on missions to escort B-17 and B-24 bombers and to bomb and strafe ground targets. At twenty-seven years old, George was considered elderly by his fellow fighter pilots, so they called him "Dad Rarey." Based in England, he flew with the 379th Fighter Squadron, 362nd Fighter Group, from February 8 to June 27, 1944. Damon, his son, knows his father through his wartime letters and cartoons.

I grew up with the World War II cartoon journals my father left. He was killed when I was three months old, and we never met, but from his daily cartoons of the Air Force base I learned much of his wonderful approach to life, as well as how to draw! Now I earn my living as an artist (computer graphics). My cartooning style and my handwriting looks like my father's. I can see that in many ways I modeled myself on what I early understood of his personality.

The other, by far greater, source of impressions of my father came from my mother, who did not stint with her memories of him. His wartime letters to her are unaffected tributes of wit and love.

Add to this the fact that my father's best friend came back from the war and married my mother when I was two, becoming another fond source of my father's image.

My father was the late-born baby of a family of eight older adoring siblings in small-town (Enid) Oklahoma, a baby who grew into a happy-go-lucky, sweet-natured child and then into a gregarious, humorous, talented adult. My mother said she never saw him angry, save once when boarding a bus a man shoved his crippled cousin (and close friend) out of the way.

A beautiful legacy, one that I had some problems relating to during a period in my life, because it seemed so ideal that I felt I couldn't live up to it. But always I came back to the drawings—there he was in a form so concrete, so gracefully goofy, so knowing and affectionate towards human foibles. Humor can't seem lofty because it depends on a contrast between what could be and what is!

Recently Ann Mix and the AWON helped me contact the surviving members of my father's squadron, men and their wives who remember him, my mother and even me from fifty years ago, people with whom we'd had no contact with since the war. I photocopied and distributed the cartoon journals of the 379th fighter squadron. In response I've received an outpouring of recollections about my father from the men (as well as some of their wives who were present during flight training in the U.S.), a wealth of new perspectives on the man who has most influenced me. One of the pilots who flew on his wing on his last mission was able to give me a first-hand account. All had fond, personal recollections.

To give a bit of the flavor, I'll quote from one of the more unique perspectives. One of the pilots told me on the phone, "Your dad didn't like me much because I was too eager. I'd tell the pilots not to bring any ammunition back—use it all on the damn Germans! I'd tell him, 'Dammit, George, don't fly between 4,000 and 8,000 feet without taking evasive action. They can throw everything at you there!' And he'd look at me and say, 'Kent, don't worry about me. I'll be all right.' You know, his problem was he really couldn't believe somebody was trying to kill him! He had no concept of that.

They shouldn't send people like that to fight wars. He was too nice. He was no warrior. He was just doing a job that had to be done. They should send people like me—50 missions and not a scratch!"

I'm deeply appreciative of my mother's generosity in sharing my dad, especially when I hear stories of legacies cut off by confusion, denial or accident. My mother's tragedy was double, because my stepfather, who continued to fly as a test pilot, was killed in the plane he was testing when I was nine, leaving also a four-year-old daughter, my sister, Courtney. My mother remarried again, had three more sons, and now lives near me and my family in Northern California. She is a survivor in the best sense and a delightful companion. We are all going to the 379th squadron reunion next year and will meet some of these folks face-to-face. My thanks to Ann Mix for putting me on the right track in finding the survivors. My only regret is that I didn't find her earlier when more of them were still around.

From the day of Dad Rarey's induction through his flight training in the United States to his voyage to Britain in the *Queen Elizabeth*, he sent a stream of letters and cartoons to Betty Lou, his fiancée and later wife. Collectively, his journals serve as a poignant example and reminder of the individuals who made up the fathers who did not return.

Always expressed with a deft hand and a gentle yet incisive wit, Rarey's communications often chronicled those unique experiences and accoutrements of military life:

"Nissen" as in Nissen hut is merely the name of some misled, well-meaning individual who invented them. A Nissen is sort of a shelter (at best), sort of like an empty tomato soup can half buried in the mud with a door and two windows at either end. We live in them and scream about them, but they are pretty cozy little deals at that. Our little stove is quite a personality, about three feet high and ten inches across, cylindrical in shape. There is a small opening in the top to put in coal and an equally small opening in the bottom to take out ashes. On the surface this coal-to-ashes cycle sounds quite simple. But not so. The stove is not equipped with a grate and successful operation requires patience and cunning with a dash of luck.

The day is putting its flaps down for its final approach, and the boys are busying themselves with various tasks near a soldier's heart. Bill is sewing on a button and bragging about a cold shower he once took. Houghton is in the sack reading a purple mystery novel. Putnam sharpens a hunting knife, while Larsen's heavy regular breathing indicates that he is in the arms of Morpheus (purely platonic, you may be sure). A variety of subjects are being aired, the air being pale blue with the mild expletives that are necessary in hitching the articles and prepositions together in an airman's banter.

Among the military problems that Rarey found in England was the fact that the squadron had arrived but their airplanes had not. Thus, much of a rainy December 1943 was spent in ground school.

Another day of nothing in particular. Lordy, but we'd like to have some airplanes! We're learning a lot but we miss the flying quite a bit. Today was typical—here it is. As far as breakfast was concerned, we were in the weeds because we grabbed an extra thirty minutes of sacktime. Our first class was at 9:00. They are informal affairs, these classes. Lectures by experienced men in our Air Force as well as the R.A.F. Interesting. At 12:00 we knocked off for lunch which consisted in a sort of hash, potatoes, and I forget what else. After about an hour of loafing around the fire in the lounge, back to the old schoolroom. Class was interrupted when a Mosquito night fighter gave us a good buzz job. That is a beautiful aircraft. We got quite a thrill out of it. I'm beginning to feel like a groundpounder. Sure will feel good to feel that old prop pulling you along again. I didn't realize how much I could miss flying. School was out at 4:00. Threw on a blouse and then to dinner after two bottles of very good ale in the lounge.

They have issued us English bicycles—they are fine vehicles and we have a lot of fun riding in formation, etc. They will never, however, take the place of the airplane—the main drawback being that they are too dangerous.

Later, Rarey's letters and cartoons would joke about the new German wonder weapon, the V-1 "buzz bombs."

I suppose you've read of the pilotless aircraft Germany has developed. It's an amazing thing aeronautically speaking but is proving rather ineffective as a weapon. We get quite a kick out of them. They are referred to as "The Doodlebug" or the Sears Roebuck job. And Tom Liston dubbed them "Those nonunion aircraft."

Rarey primarily centered his attention, however, on his beloved Betty Lou and the upcoming birth of their first child. His infatuation with both was manifest.

Betty Lou, we've had some obstacles before, but this is the supreme test. Remember the beautiful hours on your back steps and the little 15th Street studio. That place wasn't big enough to hold my happiness—even with the big window open. I've loved you there and in a thousand other places. And, Betty Lou, I love you here— more than ever before. Two lives happily intermingled, impatient with the barrier of great distances, impatient with this tremendous war, anxious to be finished with it so that we can do the things we want to do. I want to live with you, Betty Lou, with you and our boy or girl. I want to live with you and love you for the next forty-three-thousand years. I like to lie in my sack in the dark and just let my mind dance over the fine years, the innumerable happy little incidents we've shared. Oh, you rascal, I love you.

I thoroughly agree with your idea of a perfect Sunday—late sack—leisurely, fat breakfast—funnies—naps—snacks—and smooching. That last I could do a lot of. I wonder if we'll ever catch up with the lovemaking we're missing. No—I suppose we can never really catch up but I'll bet we break some records trying—raroooooo!

. . . Is it proper for an old married fellow to be so in love with his wife? . . . As you mentioned, our sense of values has been tempered in the heat of one hell of a big war. This time apart will show the value of little things that one might take for granted.

I usually refer to our little stranger (who isn't a stranger) as a boy. This is not wishful thinking, Betty Lou—a little girl would be fine. I do it as a matter of convenience. I will *not* [emphasis in original] refer to our child as an "it" or a "little thing." Even though the sex is undetermined, I'll wager the personality that will later make him or her the toast of the new generation is in full flower—a very remarkable child. How's that for a preview of true paternal understatement—just practicing.

As 1944 began, Rarey wrote Betty Lou:

Happy New Year, Mama—1944 will go down in history as the year in which Betty Lou and Rarey's first child saw the light of day— I hope it will also be marked by the destruction of Fascism in Germany and the rest of Europe. I hope our child has a chance to contribute his two cents' worth of light and color to this battered old world without being swept up in one of these mechanized free-for-alls. This war seems incidental because it's already started and has begun to exhaust itself. The vital thing is to get and keep the goddamn thing straightened out long enough for all the children to come to bat—not with two strikes on them but with a clear field. Hadn't noticed that I was winding up in a sermon—fo'give me.

We went to town New Year's Eve and checked several pubs. Stayed at the Red Cross Officers' Club all night and fooled around in town on New Year's Day. It was a pretty melancholy little brawl— all of us homesick. When the crowd raised their drunken voice in "Auld Lang Syne" I could have wept. With you here it would have been a different story.

With the arrival of their aircraft and the completion of final training, the squadron flew its first mission on February 8, 1944. When weather permitted, Rarey now found himself often flying two missions a day as the Allies moved closer to D-Day.

I'll be glad to get home, Betty Lou. We'll sit on the porch in the summer, just resting and talking and maybe having a tall, cool one. God! It'll be good to live like a human being instead of doubling for the brains of a goddamned airplane. Pay it no mind, child, the old man just let down his hair. I miss you so very much. I miss you and the life we've lived together. I want to sit across a table from you in one of our favorite places and eat and talk and just watch you. I want to touch your hair and kiss you on your lovely mouth. I want long evenings with you filled with things we like together, long nights, cigarettes together, your love and warmth. I dream of these things. I want to wake up and see you there and I want to have breakfast with you and begin a full, wonderful day together, the days following one after the other with no interruptions, just two happy people and their beautiful child and their love. I can wait, Betty Lou, as long as necessary but, God, I'd like to see you—stay with it, Betty Lou, this war isn't exactly going backwards.

For Rarey, the approaching birth of their child filled more and more of his thoughts and drawings.

Dear Betty Lou—Is it time for the expectant father to start getting panicky? Maybe I'm premature, but, pal, I get weak as hell when I think of the time approaching. I'm there with you, darling, every minute. It's probably a good thing that I'm not there in person, because I'd be an awful bother—I'm a sissy where such things are concerned. When I get back home you must spare me no details of the phenomenon of the birth of a baby. I think it's the most wonderful thing in the world. Do you realize that you are practically a mother? What an unnecessary observation on my part. You are the official

Madonna of the 379th and our child has the finest bunch of uncles that ever rolled an airplane.

Finally came the day.

Betty Lou, this happiness is nigh unbearable. Got back from a mission at 4:00 this afternoon and came up to the hut for a quick shave before chow. What did I see the Deacon waving at me as I walked up the road to the shack? A small yellow envelope! I thought it was a little early but I quit breathing completely until the wonderful news was unfolded. A son! Darling, Betty Lou! How did you do it? I'm so proud I'm beside myself! All of the boys in the squadron went wild. I had saved my tobacco ration for the last two weeks and had obtained a box of good American cigars. Old Doc Finn trotted out two quarts of Black and White from his medicine chest, and we all toasted the fine new son and his beautiful mother. What a ridiculous and worthless thing a war is in the light of such a wonderful event. That there will never be war for Damon!

Rarey followed the next day with this letter.

May I compliment you, Madame, on your wonderful courage. You carried the whole thing off beautifully. As we Englandicized Anglo-Saxons say, "Good show, my deah, cheahs!" I mean it, Betty Lou. I'm awfully proud of you. Now I'm in possession of a few facts—8 pounds, 6 ounces—what a man! What a husky little brute!—I hope you had an easy time of it. . . . Gator Kline flew up to Scotland to get us some scotch. They didn't have any so he brought back 36 quarts of rum in his belly tank (no foolin').

Do you know, Betty Lou, that Damon will be the only member of the second generation in the 379th Fighter Squadron? I hope he feels his responsibility—I suppose we could consider him in preflight. Wait 'till he gets his wings. How I should love to see you and that little rascal Damon (Gosh, I like that name!). I'm so lucky to have such a fine gal for a partner in this strange business of founding a dynasty. There are so many things I look forward to—Damon and his friends, playing and working with him, teaching him things and learning things from him. Through it all, you are there, the master wheel in the wonderful planless plan. I'm forced to take a rather sophisticated view of the political and economical future of the world—but if we can get this business of Fascism knocked off and get the world into some semblance of order and keep it there for a time, Damon and his contemporaries will take over and make something really good out of it. We're learning, but a great many mistakes will be made before a really good world order will evolve. If we can clear the air for Damon and his generation, we're fat! And that is the last word I have on geo-politics—I'm getting positively stuffy.

The arrival of the first photographs of Damon elicited even greater joy in his absent father.

The pictures! The wonderful pictures! My mental picture of Damon has been filled in by descriptions from you. Then—little pictures—oh, happy. I've had them only about 8 hours and they are famous throughout the group. Please don't think I bore these guys—they're fascinated. Damon always gets a good laugh, a chuckle, and a "Rarey, you lucky bastard!" not addressed to Damon but to his pa. You, Betty Lou, get a long, low whistle and I get one more, "Rarey, you lucky bastard!" You know the one of you and Damon together—well, it is now mounted in plexiglass from a wrecked airplane on my instrument panel—right between the gyro horizon and the altimeter—the three (or four, I should say) most consulted instruments in the whole airplane.

Damon and his friends will flock to our house. They'll love his mother and put up with his old man because he'll make sling shots and kites for them and tell them tall stories about the great war. I come from a long uninterrupted line of family men, Betty Lou, and I plan to carry on in the old Rarey tradition, even if I have been interrupted a bit by this small but vigorous global fracas. Interrupted Rarey, they calls me.

Betty Lou, tell our son to stick by his guns—only sane people sleep all night. The beautiful night was made for loving, thinking, and talking—and sleep should be the by-product of living. Unfortunately, the war here is fought principally in the daytime.

I would certainly like to see you and old Damon in action. I guess a little guy like that is pretty much of a problem, sort of like a gross little old cadet during his first few hours in primary [flight training], helpless and sort of messy.

Rarey sent his last letter on June 26, 1944.

Dear Betty Lou—Just got a V-mail and an air mail from you. They were fine. That anniversary letter was mighty sweet. We are a lucky pair, darling. We'll never be behind the door when the happiness is passed out. There wasn't a great deal of activity today due to weather. We slept late and loafed around. . . . Lord, Betty Lou, it seems like an eternity since I've seen you—since last November in that fine little world of ours—I hated to leave it. I don't care for this war—I want you and Damon and the life of our own choosing. I want to worry about the bills—ho! ho!—and mow the lawn and make kites and stuff for the demon and his friends. I want to see you and kiss you every day of my life—I want to beef about your silly hats and tell you how lovely you are. I've got all these things to do and time's a-wastin'—I ain't getting any younger, neither! So let's get the war over—okay? "Until that happy day, you know damned well, I can't give you anything but love letters, baby." Silly, isn't it? You just keep that old light in your eyes (and the one in the window) and we'll be fat. Ah, I love you my sweet Betty Lou.

The next day, the weather cleared. Rarey, flying his P-47 that he had named and decorated "Damon's Demon," led a flight of four aircraft that spotted German trucks along a French road. As they dove to attack, German anti-aircraft guns erupted, and Rarey's aircraft disintegrated when it received a direct hit. Rarey died instantly. His body is among the ten thousand dead buried at the American cemetery that today overlooks Omaha Beach.

Mamie Frantz Rarey, Damon's grandmother, recalled her son's special spirit and joy through these words:

"But it isn't playing the game," he said
And slammed his books away—
"The Latin and Greek I've got in my head
Will do for a duller day."
"Rubbish!" I cried
"The bugle call isn't for lads from school!"
D'ye think he'd listen? Ah, not at all,
So I called him a fool—a fool!

Now there's his dog by his empty bed
At Georgetown where we often went
And his favorite bat—but my boy is dead
Somewhere in Europe, they say.
My boy! With his rapture of song and sun!
My boy! Of the light brown hair—
My boy! Whose life had just begun with his own little son
Under a cross out there!

Look at his prizes, all in a row
Medals that hint of fame.
Now it's all over—we miss him so!
Doesn't it seem a shame?
A fool? Ah no! He was more than wise.
His was the proudest part.
He died with the glory of faith in his eyes
And the glory of love in his heart.[1]

---

[1]AWON files and Damon Frantz Rarey, ed., *Laughter and Tears: A Combat Pilot's Sketchbook of World War II Squadron Life: The Art of Captain George Rarey* (Santa Ross, CA: Vision Books International, 1996).

Captain George Rarey, Spring 1944, Headcorn, County Kent, England.

Betty Lou Rarey (now Kratoville), with son Damon, circa June 1944, Washington, D.C.

George Rarey's sketch commemorating the birth of his son, Damon Rarey. In a letter to his wife on this date, he says: "What a ridiculous and worthless thing a war is in the light of such a wonderful event. That there would be no war for Damon!"

One of George Rarey's sketches depicting ground school lectures in England. December 1943.

One of Rarey's last sketches, circa June 1944, of his wife Betty Lou. His letter to her on June 26 reads "We are a lucky pair, darling. . . . I want you and Damon and the life of our own choosing. I want to worry about the bills and mow the lawn and make kites and stuff for the demon and his friends. . . . I've got all these things to do and time's a wastin.'"

A self-portrait by George Rarey, December 1943.

Ellen:

We Were Isolated and Very Different, and I Knew It

*E*llen's father, William Kermit Jones, was from Bluefield, West Virginia, a rail town west of the New River along the Virginia-West Virginia state line. William, usually called by his middle name Kermit, had two brothers and two sisters. When war came, all three brothers volunteered for service. Even though Kermit had already married Ellen's mother Hope, he entered the Army Air Force. He was on a troop train headed for training in San Antonio, Texas, when Ellen was born. He saw her twice before he left for Europe. While he served overseas, Ellen and her mother lived in Virginia on her family's farm with Hope's sister and Ellen's cousins.

Kermit served as a gunner in an A-26 Invader, a speedy twin-engine bomber used for bombing at medium altitudes and for strafing and bombing at low levels. Kermit was part of the Ninth Air Force, 409th Bombardment Group, 642d Bombardment Squadron. Cursed by chronic sinus problems that often sent him to sick bay, he could have escaped flying duty altogether but chose not to do so. In a letter to a sister in early January 1945, he talked·about his combat duty:

Well, Sugar, naturally you wonder about my missions. I'll tell you that so far I've been lucky. Sometimes the flak comes close, mighty close. But for the most part the missions are comparatively easy. They are cold, damn! It gets so cold up there the air looks blue, and so does everything else—including myself. But when we come back, and go to interrogation for questioning, we get hot coffee, doughnuts, and sometimes a slug of good U.S.A. "Likker." Then we leave for chow, a wash, and to the sack (bed). I guess the prettiest sight a gunner can ever see is the P-38s, 47s and 51s,[1] and sometimes a Spitfire (British) comes wagging up, flashin' them pretty wings at us. It's a good feeling.

For the most part we live outdoors. Our home is a tent, and now we have a mess hall which was finished Christmas. And we have a kitchen too. It's fairly warm in the tent as long as the fire is going, but when it goes down at night it is almost the same as sleeping outside, except the tent does hold the moisture off of us. . . . Last year at this time I was in the hospital for a long time, and the year before too. But I'm not going to the hospital this year—not if I can help it.

Well, write to me and if there's anything you want to know, ask, and I'll try to answer it. Do you want something from Paris?

On January 23, 1945, while on a low-level attack against the German road junction of Gemünd, German anti-aircraft fire downed Kermit's bomber. He died a few days later in a German hospital.

Ellen was then three years old. She has no recollection of her father. From the beginning of her memory, she simply knew that her father was dead.

My cousin remembers that there was a sink hole on the farm, and that after my father was declared missing, or maybe after he was declared dead, a lot of the things my mother had sent [were returned]—because this was right after Christmas—so there were packages coming back that she had sent. I've often thought, why would they send that stuff back? But my cousin, who would have been five, she went with mother. Mother took this stuff to the sink hole and threw it in. It's heart-rending. . . . I was trying to remember when I knew my father was dead. I always knew. I don't remember ever being told. I always knew. . . . I don't remember anybody ever actually telling me that he was dead.

After Kermit died, Ellen's mother rarely spoke of her husband. They had only been married a short time before he left for the war. Because of her mother's silence, Ellen's only source of information was Kermit's family.

I used to always drive down to Bluefield with my grandfather and I thought it was 800 miles because he was the worst driver in the world. He would take any little road and go off and investigate something, and you thought it was forever, like driving to Kansas, but it wasn't far at all. I spent almost every summer out there, not the whole summer, but a few weeks every summer.

My grandmother loved talking about my father. I think it brought him back to her, and she would smile and tell funny stories, and she really enjoyed it. My aunts and uncles, too. They talked about him, and he was real. So I always felt like he was there. He was very funny apparently. He had a very good sense of humor. . . . I loved little anecdotes. My grandmother would say, "Well, you and your daddy would have gotten along just fine because you love cake icing and he only liked the cake." She was very good. My father was apparently the favorite. He was the youngest son. I don't know how they dealt with his death. I think they were just devastated, but at least he wasn't the only one. She talked about him and he was real. So I always felt like he was there.

About the only thing my mother has ever said is that he was the sweetest man she ever knew, which doesn't mean much when you're trying to get a picture of somebody. But my aunts and uncles are much better at that because they were his peers. My mother knew him as a boyfriend and lover, and didn't know him for that long or see him that much. They weren't together that much. I guess most of their life was in letters.

My father used to have lots of pictures taken of himself and sent home. He was very handsome. They all used to laugh about how he was forever giving people pictures of himself. But now they're all so glad he did.

My grandmother made my father real for me. My mother and I never talked about him much, but he was always there. It was very important. You probably gain some strength from that, although I don't remember ever consciously—I guess you couldn't make the connection to say, "This is what my father would want me to do," or "This is a bad thing. My father wouldn't want me to do that." You wouldn't go that far, but still you had the sense of that person. Yes, I did have this feeling that God the Father and my father were there together. There was a peculiar thing. I don't know how to put it into words, but it was very strange.

My grandparents had my dad's dog, a German shepherd who didn't like some people at all, but liked my mother and me very much. When they put me down for a nap, Flops would lie across the bedroom door so I couldn't be disturbed. The family thought he sensed my connection with my father. Flops let me hang onto the fur on his back and pull myself up; then he would walk very slowly. That's how I learned to walk.

Along with her family's stories and photos and Flops, a recording also played its part in recalling her father.

My father's family is very political, and I had a record. I actually heard his voice. I used to love playing this record. They were discussing politics and the war. It was before Pearl Harbor, and my grandmother and grandfather and my father were talking about Roosevelt. My grandfather hated Roosevelt. They were talking about him and the war in Europe and the economy and all that stuff. Then, on the other side of the record, he liked to play the piano, and he was playing "Moonlight Sonata." I had it for years. I don't know what I did with it; it's gone. I had it when it was important to me. I used to play it a lot. That was all. That was the best you could do.

Then somebody once told me his favorite song was—it's real corny, but I loved it for years—"Bluebird of Happiness." What was his name, that opera singer? Jan Peerce. And I had it, and for years I would play it. Then, after I finished college and started working, sometimes I would sit and drink wine and get drunk and put on "Bluebird of Happiness." Very emotional stuff. Things I never talked to other people about. I have never told people these things. It is just me, it is just my little thing. Nobody else would understand unless they had been through it.

Conversations with Ellen's mother were less easy and rich than with her grandmother.

Sometimes I did want to talk to my mother about him, but I just felt it was not good to do it. But it was embarrassing because it was awkward. Maybe it was just so emotional that it hurt her to discuss it. My mother was much better at describing how a baby is born and drawing a uterus than she was in telling me about my father who was dead.

Mother never talked about him much. She would tell me a couple little things now and then, but it was very awkward and I never knew what to call him. I would say "my father." It was even hard to say that. It was very uncomfortable. It was almost embarrassing in a way. Whenever it would come up, that I had to mention anything about him, I didn't know what to call him, and so it was very strange. So I would say "my father."

My cousins and I grew up like sisters. We were all together on our mothers' family farm during the war, but their father came home and mine didn't. Mother and I moved away from the farm . . . but my cousins and I stayed close, which is good since I have no brothers and sisters. I remember one time, when we had been to church and my cousins and I were out in the driveway playing. And I started singing this hymn, "This Is My Father's World." And my cousin said, "You can't sing that," because, I guess, she knew I didn't have a father. She was taking it literally. I said, "Why not? I don't know why not." I just remember really pushing her to tell me why I couldn't sing it.

I remember when I was in grammar school. I just cringe thinking about it now, but you know how you didn't want to be different from everybody else, but you were because you didn't have a father and they did. Well the principal came to our class. There was a Jones Taxi Service in Staunton [Virginia], and he asked me if my father owned it and I said, "He's dead." I said it as if it was a joke, "He's DAYED." I was just embarrassed. I don't think I ever told my mother. But I hated it. I remember hating it. That was hard. It was a small town and everybody knew anyway.

My mother had this burden—you have this child that you have to raise alone, at least for part of it, unless you married again. I always felt she was glad to have me, except one time when I set the dining room curtains on fire. And now she has gotten old she likes to tell the story in this sweet way, as if I were lighting candles for the Little Christ Child, except I wasn't. I was lighting matches and wanted to see if this curtain would burn, and it did. I didn't burn the house down. I just burned the curtains but she was real upset.

I guess there are plenty of kids whose fathers die in automobile accidents, and then we have kids in Washington, D.C., today whose fathers are being killed and killed and killed. So I guess, if anything, we're lucky that it happened in some meaningful way, because you always have that to cling to. You didn't have to think how useless it was. So that could carry you through. So it was okay to be sad about it, but you could be very proud, except that you were usually the only one in town. And no kids wants to be—I just remember feeling like I didn't want to be different, and I was always different for that reason. Even though nobody discussed it, I knew I was, although it was much easier when I was with my grandparents and with people who talked about him a lot because then it was like there was no difference. I wasn't unusual. Because even if you knew things about your father, you didn't really discuss him, you didn't really say those things to your little friends because they were uncomfortable about it, too.

Since World War II was her father's world, Ellen had a special interest in the war as she grew up. It could be a way of being with him. Within that place, however, she had to deal with an occasional tinge of anger that her father had volunteered to fly and, thus, had knowingly run the risk of not returning to her.

I grew up thinking my father was a hero and that it was a good war and that he died for a cause and that it wasn't without reason. I did dwell on the war a lot. I read a lot about it. I had books about it. I liked to go to movies about World War II. I liked all that stuff, which is unusual for girls. I wanted to know all about it.

My father volunteered. He wasn't drafted. [He] probably didn't have to [fly]. Every now and then I think I should be irritated with him for that. Why would he do that? But everybody in my [father's] family was [in the war]—and I used to be very proud of that point too, that everybody in the family—he was the only one that got killed. Even my Aunt Ellen was an Army nurse.

Although as an adult she rarely mentioned her status as a war orphan, occasionally her emotions bubbled to the surface.

This is bad. I was at a dinner party with a few people, and the German wife—these were all dental students at Georgetown, and one of them had a German wife. I have no idea why [I said it]—I had just been to Germany I guess. My friend kind of dragged me, kicking and screaming, through Germany, because they would say things like, "There used to be a church on this corner, but the Americans bombed it," and I would be thinking of my father. It was terrible, and I had to work through this prejudice. Anyway, this woman was talking . . . about the Germans. She said, "But Hitler did some good things. He built the Autobahn and the Volkswagen," and she was trying to take up for Hitler. I couldn't imagine anybody doing that. And I said, "'Yes, and he killed my father." Normally, I never said things like that. I must have had something to drink.

Such instances, however, were a rarity. Instead, as with so many war orphans, Ellen learned as a child to keep her thoughts and emotions to herself.

We were very isolated and very different, and I knew it. So in that way we were orphans. Orphans probably [lived by the rule] "fit in as best you can and don't talk about it, and maybe nobody will notice." I don't know, but it did [feel that way]. "Don't make waves." Maybe some other person will know why their mother wouldn't talk about it. It could have been just this thing of let's put that behind us and go on. We have to go on, and we don't remember this because it's sad, it hurts. And a grownup wouldn't need to remember it. I mean, particularly if they married again, but my mother went on with her life and dated, even though she never married again. I guess you wouldn't realize what a child was feeling, that a child wanted to know the answers to all these questions. I wonder why my grandmother knew. Mothers wanted to go ahead. They were focused on the future, and they didn't want to go back, and that was so painful. It was just so painful. It was like opening a door they had closed and didn't want to ever open again. It's probably more that than anything else. I don't know if they didn't think we needed to know or if there was just no way to tell us. They would have no way to tell us what life could have been like, because they didn't know. They could only tell us facts.

I don't remember ever resenting it or feeling upset about it particularly, but I used to sort of dream about it. It was just sort of a daydream. How things could have been.[2]

---

[1] American fighter planes often used to escort bombers.
[2] Interview with Susan Hadler, September 26, 1993; letter of Kermit Jones to Elizabeth Jones, January 5, 1945; AWON files.

Elizabeth Ellen Jones (left) and cousins Louise Martin (center) and Carolyn Martin (right) living together with their mothers on a farm in the Shenandoah Valley, Virginia, the winter of 1944–45.

William Kermit Jones and Hope Ervine Jones at Virginia Polytechnic Institute circa 1941.

Elizabeth Ellen Jones at four years of age, 1946.

William Kermit Jones, Gunner,
642nd Bombardment Squadron,
409th Bombardment Group (L). Shot
down 23 January 1945, died circa 8
February 1945.

Hope Ervine Jones and Elizabeth
Ellen Jones, October 1942.

Gunners' briefing, 1944–45, Bretigny, France. William Kermit Jones is standing in
the last row, second from right.

Clint:
How Was It That We Didn't Count?

$\mathcal{C}$lint's father, Captain George Frederick, died on March 30, 1944, and is buried in the Philippines. A pilot, he was serving as an air liaison officer with ground units when a Japanese sniper killed him on the small island of Pityilu, a dot in the Admiralty chain. The island sits just north of the main island of Manus. He had been overseas for just under a year. When his father died, Clint was not quite five months old. Captain Frederick had never seen his son but had written this letter to his wife Cleo in July 1943:

My dearest sweet Cleo,

When you read this letter I will either be missing in action, killed or captured and the last possibility is very remote because if I have any fight left in me, I will give my life to defend not only my country but the principles on which it was founded. I want you and our children to be able to live in freedom as you want, wherever you want and to do what you want. I want the opportunity for our child to be able to grow up and to be kind, gentle, and Christian. I want our child to be able to go to school and to college to learn whatever profession he or she wants to learn.

If (our child) is a boy I want him to grow up and be a better man than his Dad. I want him to marry, if he chooses, a wife as kind and sweet as his mother. If a girl, I know she will be as fine a wife to some man as you have been to me.

You will wonder why I have written this. I wonder myself, but last night I lay thinking. "What if I should be killed, would Cleo know what my mind was thinking as to our future?" I have no premonition of being killed, and am trusting in the Lord to watch over me and keep me safe, but when He calls I will be ready.

It is a nice feeling, to know that whatever happens to me, I will meet you again someday, but in a home that will be far nicer than any we could ever have had here on earth. So don't grieve, just think that I have gone away for a little while and I'll see you again.

Farewell my darling until we meet again.

George

Clint and his mother lived for a time on his grandparents' farm in the southeastern corner of Kansas:

My grandparents were great. The childhood though was kind of rough for a couple of reasons. One was that in 1945, within the year after my father being killed, the house that we lived in burned down. All mementos, or anything my mother had concerning my father, were destroyed. However, a trunk of his clothes did arrive after the house burned down, so I did get his trunk with his uniform and some effects, which was great.

One day Clint's grandmother was making soap. "I reached out and grabbed some and ate it. I was two years old. It was liquid lye soap, and I took a handful of it. It was kind of mushy, and I ate some of it. The soap went down and burned my esophagus." Clint spent the next two years in a hospital.

Through the fourth grade, he attended a rural one-room school. When his mother moved to Pittsburg, Kansas, to take college classes, Clint attended a city school for the first time. He did not mix easily with his class-mates.

I always felt that I was somewhat of a loner. Possibly because of my mother's activities in church and my going to Sunday School, and what not, and because of my having [eaten] the lye soap, when it came to getting into fights, which kids will do, I would avoid them. I should have just gone ahead and fought and been a boy, but I wasn't. I felt as a result of avoiding fights I was somewhat picked on. They said things like, "Yeah, your father was a big war hero but you're sure not!" That type of thing. The other problem was that I was born in November so I was just about the youngest one in my class and I was also the smallest. I should have been held back a grade, I am fully convinced now.

Although Clint hoped that his mother would remarry, she was reluctant. It would be forty years after her husband's death before she took that step. In addition, Clint was troubled by having to live up to the memory of his heroic father.

My mother, she always had these very high standards. I always felt like I had to live up to the image of my father. This was an impossible task because of her feelings about him, that he could do no wrong. She didn't remarry until about ten years ago [1984]. She always talked about what a neat person my dad was and the reason she didn't remarry, which I always wanted her to do, was because she was very, very picky. Even though she dated some men who were really fine they just didn't live up to the qualities my father had. They were not good enough.

She did have one steady boyfriend who she went with for about three or four years, and I thought they were going to get married. But they didn't. He ended up marrying somebody else, and I got very upset about that. It just totally tore my mother up, really, really bad. I was so mad I did a stupid thing. I had my father's .45 automatic pistol and I loaded that thing up and I went to go see him. I was going to shoot the son of a bitch, but I didn't do it because he wasn't there.

She is remarried now to a really fine person. He has been really good to her. We aren't really as close as maybe she would like. I like to have some distance between me and her. I would rather be myself. We aren't all that close as maybe we once were. She gives me the impression of being disapproving in one way or another of something I am doing. She wants to know about my business or something and she seems to be looking for something she can be really proud of, like when I give a talk or speech or something. She wants to know all about it and asks me maybe two thousand questions. But I would still get the impression that, hey, this was not good enough because maybe there were only a hundred people and she wants one hundred thousand [laughs]. I think she wants me to be something that I can never be. At the same time part of it was me, too. I tied her hands. For example, when I got sick. She still makes a big deal about what all she had to go through. I was a big burden to her. At the same time she is really happy that she had that burden.

Reflecting on his adult life (he has been married twice) and his own role as a father, Clint observes:

I think I could have been a *lot* better father [emphasis in original]. I devoted too much of my time to work and my career. I thought number one was my job. I should have spent a lot more time being more family oriented. I was raised without a father image or a figure as to what a father should be. I could have done a lot better.

I live on the edge. If I have a dime I'll spend it. I have never been able to save money. I am a risk taker, a gambler in many ways, risky stocks, lottery tickets. I smoked and drank to the point where I can't do that anymore. . . . I always drove very fast. My last ticket was in Iowa for going 95 in a 65 zone.

One thing about us war orphans, we did not have the earning power of our fathers to assist financially in our lives. They weren't there to help us with a loan for our first home or anything like that.

My mother didn't have any of these resources. But she ended up giving me the checks that she received from the government every month for an allowance. They were $36.00. I didn't inherit from my father's family either. There is something there that needs to be looked into that was universal. How was it that we didn't count?[1]

[1]Interview with Ann Mix, June 6, 1995; letter from George to Cleo, July 1943; AWON files.

George F. Frederick and his future wife Cleo N. Campbell, June 1942. Pittsburg, Kansas.

Captain George F. Frederick was killed in action on 30 March 1944 on the island of Pitylu in the Admiralty Islands off the coast of New Guinea.

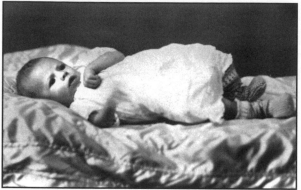

George Clinton Frederick ("Clint"), the day he left the
hospital after surgery. January 1944, Pittsburg, Kansas.

Clint Frederick, 5 years old, in Pittsburg, Kansas.

Clint and his mother lived with her parents on their farm for a
few years, and even after moving away spent a lot of time there.
Clint is on the right. Circa 1952.

Ann:
Every Memory Is Bittersweet

$\mathcal{M}$y most cherished memories of my father, Sydney Bennett, are buried under a pile of painful memories and craziness. To remember my father, I must internally walk back through what seems like a corridor of confusing experience. Every memory is bittersweet, the good times tempered by the fact that they all lead to the eventual death of my father and my life after he died. The good times and the beautiful visions I have of my father can never be accessed without accessing my loss. So, in effect, even the wonderful things have been tainted or destroyed, like a love affair that ends too soon, leaving one with the explosion that comes at the end, destroying everything that came before the parting. It is hard to be comforted by the fact that there were good times.

They say a little girl's first romantic love is with her father. This was certainly true in my case. When my father entered our house in Bakersfield, California, the whole world lighted up. He was outgoing and funny. His physical appearance contributed to his funniness. Besides having a terrific sense of humor and a desire to make people laugh, he was skinny and tall and gangly and kind of goofy looking. He enjoyed music and loved to sing and whistle, and sometimes he played the saxophone. My mother played the piano and the accordion. When family and friends came by, which they often did, we stood around the piano and sang.

My dad had lots of friends. His best friend was his brother Jim. They relished playing cards and pool and drinking beer. I recall my brother, Sydney, and I going to father's favorite pool hall to find him and being given a nickel for a frosty ice cream and then being sent home. Wherever he was we wanted to be. Once, waiting for him, I fell asleep on the passenger-side running board of his car, and he took off down the road with me. Someone saw me and flagged him down.

Although I have happy memories, I have the dark memories, too. The war was always with us. We lived with my dad's mother, and over the breakfast table Father and Grandmother read the newspaper and talked about politics and other cultures. She had traveled widely with her oilman husband and had lived in Burma. Grandmother was Father's favorite person to talk to in the whole world. My mother just sat quietly and stared out the window. She always said my dad had "big ideas." A lot of the talk centered on the war and what was happening and if my father would be called up. There was this dark cloud that hung over us.

When the news came that the Selective Service had eliminated the III-A status and the government was going to draft married men and fathers, a pall descended over our home. By May of 1944, my father was drafted even though he had two children and a widowed mother who depended on him. He was twenty-six years old. I was only three and a half, but I remember.

Before we knew what was happening, he was gone to boot camp. When I saw my dad again, he had been transformed into a soldier with a duffel bag. His new clothes, his spit-shined shoes, the creased hat folded flat on his knee, were all different. We had to investigate everything the Army gave him, including his mess kit and how it came apart. Although he showed off his Army gear, his demeanor was not the same. He had never seemed so serious.

Before he left, he went to Taft, near Bakersfield, where Grandma was now staying, to say goodbye to her. My cousin Beverly told me a few years ago that they spent hours together in her bedroom, behind closed doors. Beverly was playing hymns, the only songs she knew, on the piano. My grandmother was a devout Christian and was pleading with my father to accept Christ as his savior before he left for the war. He apparently was terribly anguished about this and, hearing the hymns, yelled out, "Does she have to keep playing those god-damned hymns!" No one knows for sure what transpired in that bedroom, but Beverly believes he finally got on his knees and prayed with his mother. When I was given the box with his effects, I found a well-worn Bible and a church lapel pin.

The next morning, he left in the dark for Los Angeles where he boarded a train for the east. We were not allowed to go, and his mother was too sick to make the trip. My mother was the only one there to see him off. Before he left, he came to the day bed on which my brother Syd and I slept. He was crying and told Sydney to take care of my mother and me, and he told me to be a good girl. Then he was gone. He made one stop in Chicago where he visited with my mother's brother at the train stop. He asked Delmar to watch out for us kids if anything happened to him. He told my uncle he didn't think he was going to make it through the war.

He was shipped out and was sent to a replacement depot in Italy. He was pulled in as a replacement during heavy fighting and joined the 87th Mountain Infantry Regiment, which was part of the 10th Mountain Division. He was in combat three days before he was killed, nineteen days before the Germans surrendered and the war in Europe ended.

He died in the small northern Italian village of Mongiorgio around 10:00 in the morning. He was killed by a German sniper's bullet to the neck as he entered a clearing. He died almost instantly.

When we received word that he was killed, my mother took us to his sister's house. Grandma was in a green wicker rocking chair, keening and crying. Everyone was worried about her, and the first question asked when anyone arrived was about how she was doing. My uncle and aunts were all crying too. There is no crying in the world like that of someone who has just received such terrible news. It is an ocean. My brothers and I were surrounded and swept up in this ocean of grief with no adult able to support or care for us. Sydney was six and a half. I was four and a half, and my younger brother Tom, born after my father left, was only four months old. Sydney took me by the hand and led me away to take care of me as he had been told to do. He was now the man of the house. We went off to wander in the spring day, not knowing what to think or what to do. He explained to me that our father had died for his country, that he was a hero. His was the only explanation I ever had. Shortly after that I remember telling someone who came to the house that my dad killed Hitler; maybe Sydney had told me that, too.

Our mother was unhappy, she was lonely, and mostly she ignored us. She just wasn't there. We went to live with her parents; my grandfather converted a chicken coop into a little one-bedroom house for us. We called it the Little Red House because of its siding. My grandfather ruined his knees spreading concrete by himself for the floor in that little house. His knees were running sores and he would come in and sit in a chair and Grandmother would tend to them, but he continued until the house was done.

My grandfather was a tough German carpenter who never showed emotion. But years later when my brother Tom went to Vietnam and came to say goodbye to him, my grandfather cried. He was the only man in our family who was involved with us after my father died.

My mother seemed desperate to remarry and she went out with a lot of men. She began to drink heavily. I remember the first time I saw her drunk. She was staggering and asking my grandmother where her pajamas were. My grandmother said, "You fool, you're drunk. You already have them on!"

She met Jim Smith, a former Marine, in a bar. When she brought him home the first time and he sat down in a chair, I ran over to him, jumped in his lap, and hugged him and said, "Will you be my daddy?" He was half Indian and had a round, brown face. I remember patting his cheeks and feeling as though I just couldn't snuggle close enough to him. He used to say that I was the reason he married my mom. Today, I believe that could partly be true. Although their marriage was fraught with alcoholism and violent fighting and they divorced ten years later, I believe his intentions were good.

Even though I now had a substitute father, I dreamed about my dad throughout my childhood. Whenever I heard a marching band, I cried. Whenever I saw the American flag waving, I got a lump in my throat. I never really knew why I felt this way. I was told my father was a hero who died for his country and for our freedom; I had a feeling that somehow I was supposed to be a hero, too. My part was to be good and to be brave.

My relationship with my mother, in regard to my father, became stranger as she became more and more disillusioned with her second marriage and as she spiraled into alcoholism. The problems I had which related to the death of my father became overshadowed by the obvious fact of her unhappy life and alcoholic behavior and its effect on me. Separating my mother and her problems, which I internalized, from my own suffering connected to my experience as an orphan, required years of counseling. For many years, I believed my own problems, including extreme self-consciousness and insecurity, free floating feelings of fear, and swinging back and forth from believing I had some ability to do something with my life to despair that I was unworthy and stupid, stemmed from my troubled relationship with my mother. This was made more difficult because the issues were so often connected.

For years my mother would come into my room in the middle of the night and wake me. She was drunk and wanted to talk about my father. I can still hear her voice and feel her finger poking me. "Annie, Annie wake up," she would repeat. Sometimes I faked sleep, but if I did she only persevered until it became impossible to pretend I was still asleep. I would roll over and she would begin. It was my father's birthday, or the anniversary of his death, or she was just thinking about him. She would cry, and I would listen. In a drunken haze, she repeated herself over and over. The sum total of this "sharing" was that she told stories over and over and fabricated a story about my father and her which, in time, she came to believe herself. It was a story that forty years later I had to take apart piece by piece in order to learn the truth. But it never occurred to me as a child that she was telling me lies, or inventing things, or creating a fantasy.

When Mother was sober, we never talked about my father. If I brought up the subject, she got angry. In fact, somewhere along the way, she burned every photo of my father and all the letters he had written when he went in the Army. When she finally admitted this, she said she did it because my stepfather was jealous of my dad's memory. I don't find this credible as Jim, my stepfather, lost two brothers in the war, and he and I talk openly about my father and my work with orphans today.

My mother made me the keeper of my father's memory when she was drunk. In her alcoholic world I was supposed to discuss him with her over and over. On the other hand, she made it impossible for me to keep his memory alive by refusing to discuss him when she was sober and by destroying his photos and letters. She also made it impossible for me to learn anything about him from his family.

Mother fought with my dad's family and told me over and over that they had robbed me of an inheritance and that I should never talk to them. She told me it would kill her if I ever talked to "those people." My father's family was educated, and she was not, and she mocked me when I talked like my father or his family and accused me of putting on airs. I had a great aunt who was the first woman doctor in Bakersfield, and even though I walked by her house every day on the way to school, I was forbidden to go there.

One day when I was in high school and was walking by, I suddenly turned up the walk to Auntie Doc's faded green wooden house, went up the creaking stairs, and with heart in my throat knocked on her door. I didn't know why I was doing that but I was full of impulses and conflicts I didn't understand.

My Auntie Doc opened the door and welcomed me with open arms. I walked into a house which was another world from the one I had been living in. The walls were lined with shelves of books and ancient Indian baskets. Everywhere there were signs of her intellect and her life's work with her patients. She was old and beautiful, with fading red hair, and granny glasses, and she walked with a cane with a handle of gold. I was trying to talk to her and drink it all in at once. Her nurse and life-time companion, Belle, was in the house, and they scurried to make me welcome and gave me tea in a china cup. I don't remember what we talked about, but when I left I ran all the way home and never told my mother what I did. In fact, I wiped that meeting from my memory as quickly as I could out of fear my mother would read my mind or somehow discern that I had been there. I never went back to see my great aunt again and closed the book on my father and his family. It wasn't until I was in my forties that I would dare to make contact with my father's family again.

Later, I went to see a sister of my father who was in a nursing home, and this time I dragged my brother Tom along with me. Again we were welcomed with opened arms and tear-filled eyes. "Oh, Tommy and Annie, I love you so much," Aunt Nota cried. We left filled with joy at seeing our aunt and rage at being deprived of her company our whole lives. This time I told my mother where I had been. We sat in her living room and she sat in a big worn-out chair with the blinds pulled against the summer heat and said nothing. She sighed. It was something she had done all my life when she was disgusted with me. Her silence was as heavy as the dust on her pulled-down blinds.

I returned home and the next time I called my mother she was too busy to come to the phone. I called back several times and she was always "busy." I finally asked my sister what was going on and she said, "Well, Ann, you just make mother feel guilty. She is like a glass doll you know, she breaks easily." I quit calling, and my mother never spoke to me again. She died two years later of cirrhosis of the liver.

In its own way, Mother's death set me free. I could now search for my father and retrieve him from the grip of her fantasies and twisted recollections. The journey to find my dad has been very much like knocking on Aunt Lois's and Aunt Nota's door, but this time I have been companioned by people that I had never known were waiting to give me a hand. This journey seems to have no end as I have found myself helping others as I have been helped by them.

All my life I wanted to go to Italy where my father died. I never felt this would be possible. I didn't have the money; I couldn't go alone; I was too afraid. But other orphans filled me with their experience and hope by sharing with me their own trips of discovery. A woman whose father is buried in Margraten, Holland, offered to buy my ticket if I would go. Susan Hadler offered to go with me. It was only because of their support and other orphans' encouragement that I found myself on an airplane flying over the mountains of Switzerland and into Italy.

As I landed in Milan, what I longed for most was to quiet my mind of the terror from imagining what had happened to my dad. I always felt and feared the awfulness of his being all alone and far from home and dying in some unfriendly, ugly war-torn land. These agonies changed when I went to Italy.

Susan and I and a new friend and guide, Walter Bellisi, drove to Mongiorgio where my father died. It was April, the same month he was killed. The climate was the same as he would have experienced in those final days. Atop a rolling mountain sits the crumbling ruin of a feudal castle and church. Slightly below it are two houses, one old and one new, built since the war. We drove up a rough narrow road to be confronted with a gate and a German shepherd dog and a do-not-enter, "danger" sign. We wandered around outside and walked back down below, exploring the place and speculating about what had transpired in Mongiorgio on that day. Suddenly a man came driving down the narrow road and stopped to greet us. Through Walter we were able to explain why we were there. The man began to talk and never stopped. He beckoned us to follow him, and we climbed the hill, wet with spring rain. He took us inside the dark damp castle where we examined everything. We saw the kitchen where the big oven for baking bread still stands, the prison, and the wheels which turned the draw bridge. Brushing aside big cobwebs and getting our clothes covered with dust we came to a room with a window where the German soldiers had stood with their guns, watching my father as he entered the clearing below. I stood where someone who killed my father stood. It was all so clear then how he died.

When we walked back down we passed through the old church which was in disarray. Piles of debris were thrown in corners. I saw some pictures in the rubble and picked one up. It was a Giovanni print of the Madonna and the Christ Child that showed dimly behind the dirty glass. I asked if I could buy it, and the man generously gave it to me. I carried it home and when I cleaned it, the original colors came through with remarkable intensity. It now hangs on my wall and reminds me of Mongiorgio.

When we went back outside and walked around the yard and looked off over the Tuscany mountains I could feel the air teeming with life and new spring flowers and budding trees. Birds sang and coasted in drafts of air in the valley below. It was the most beautiful sight I had ever seen. From the moment I landed in Italy I had been feeling something I had never felt before. I had been surrounded by loving people who smiled at me and hugged and kissed me. They patted me and cried when I cried. I had been caught up in their understanding of the horrors of war and loss. I had been basking in their embrace.

I am sure my father felt the beauty of Italy too when he came here and before he died. My cousin sent me a small photo of him sitting with his arms around an Italian girl the same age as me. She was cuddled in his embrace. How could man turn this beautiful country into a place of death? I didn't have the answer. I never will. But the Italy of my imagination had been transformed to the reality of a place that basks in golden light and is inhabited with gentle people. I stood looking away from the castle and thought, "What a beautiful place to die." Although I know that what I saw that day was not the same as when my father climbed, under fire, to the top of Mongiorgio, my heart will always be inhabited now with a country and people who were worth the sacrifice.[1]

Standing at the Alamo*

"If you are going to cry, go to the cryin' post,"
    Grandfather used to say.
He stern-fingered us to the cottonwood tree.
Rough-barked and strong, Alamo held firm for us
    as we leaned weak and weepy foreheads against his
    cracked and weathered skin.
Upon his barked breast, we mewed our woes and our
    disappointments.
Our lost innocence splashed in sparkled tears down the
    valleys of his wooden cheeks.
Once upon a time we used to grab and cry against our
    Daddy's tender leg.
But Daddy had to go to war. His chestnut eyes, his freckled
    hands, his skinny-giant legs were buried on foreign soil.
Sydney, Tom and me, we were left to grow in Grandfather's
    backyard, and to bake in the Bakersfield sun.
Grandfather offered our orphaned hearts to the
    sacred cryin'-post tree.
His wobbled-bone legs were too weak, and his
    twisted hands too torn to hold all of our broken dreams or to fill
    our empty cups.
He did what he could do, teaching us to cry standing
    in fallen Alamo leaves.
Cryin' post trees will do for fatherless children
    when Daddy's legs only brush cheeks in dreams
    that never come true.[2]

*Alamo is Spanish for a cottonwood tree

[1]Ann Bennett Mix wrote this personal history in September 1996; AWON files.
[2]Published in Caroline Sullivan, ed., *A View from the Edge* (Owings Mills, Maryland: The National Library of Poetry, Watermark Press, 1992), p. 2.

Sydney Worthington Bennett (with pipe) and unidentified buddy in Florence or Naples, 1944 or 1945.

Ted Henning, Florence Henning, Eloise Henning Bennett, and Sydney W. Bennett in 1944 in Bakersfield, California. Ted Henning and Sydney Bennett were best friends.

"In 1943, before my father was drafted, we posed for this family photo in my grandparents' front yard in Bakersfield, California. (l–r) Alberta Henning, Florence Henning, unidentified friend, Sydney Bennett, Eloise Henning Bennett, unidentified friend, Theodore Henning. Two children in front are Ann Marie Bennett and Sydney Ray Bennett.

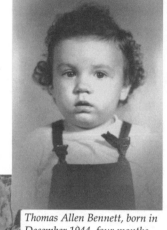

Sydney Ray Bennett (age 4) and Ann Marie Bennett (age 2) in bakersfield in 1942.

Thomas Allen Bennett, born in December 1944, four months before his father was killed.

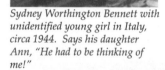

Sydney Worthington Bennett with unidentified young girl in Italy, circa 1944. Says his daughter Ann, "He had to be thinking of me!"

Ann Bennett Mix in the Florence cemetery by her father's grave, April 1996.

Clatie and John:
We Don't Know How He Died

★

★ $\mathcal{C}$latie and John are twins. Their father, Clatie Raymond Cunningham, Jr., served as a flight engineer on a B-24 bomber of the 868th Bombardment Squadron. Equipped with radar, these bombers and their ten-man crews flew primarily at night, attacking Japanese shipping and coastal targets in the area of the South China Sea. Ray, as his wife and family called him, was reported missing from a mission on July 23, 1945. His bomber had successfully attacked Japanese shipping on the Mekong River in French Indochina. Damage to the aircraft, however, forced the crew to bail out over the water. An American submarine patrolling off shore as a "life-guard" vessel picked up three crew members. The other seven crewmen, including Ray Cunningham, were never found.

As so often happens in wartime, the lack of information made the death even harder for the family. Ray's son Clatie remembers:

There was no closure about the way he died. Those survivors never saw the other guys. We don't know how he died. Sharks? Water? Drowning? Killed by the Japanese? All we know is that he went in and that they tried to rescue them.

Ray Cunningham was twenty-three years old and left behind his twenty-three-year-old wife Alice and his twin sons of less than two months. He never saw the photos of his twins.

In those days there was a time delay [before the government notified the family]. Mother wasn't notified right away. . . . Each letter that wasn't opened prior to the death was sent back. The last letter with our pictures in it was unopened.

This last letter from Alice to Ray, dated July 12, 1945, was full of love and hope for his return:

I received your two letters this afternoon. I was so glad to get them. Ray, I want you to meet your sons, Clatie Raymond III and John William. The blonde is Ray and the dark one is John. John weighs the most of the two babies. The pictures were taken just before the babies were a month old.

Darling congratulations on your S/Sgt rating. You deserve it, Darling. Please take care of that cold, Ray. Don't worry about anything and just take good care of yourself. The babies are fine and so am I. My daddy is simply crazy over the two boys and he's so proud that one of them is named after him.

Darling, I know you are just dying to see the kids. That's why I took these pictures right away. I don't look so good in the picture myself though.

Darling, I will be just looking forward for Christmas or January when you will be coming home. Darling, I am taking care of the allotment. Darling, I'll close now and will write again soon.

Margaret sat on the wet painted toilet seat today in Helen's place and got a painted ring on her bottom which was so funny. [Margaret and Helen were Alice's sisters]

All my Love,

Your Darling Wife Alice and sons Ray and John

XXXXX a million, X from Ray, X from John.

I love You. I miss You. I am glad to know that you are crazy about me.

Now alone, with infant twin sons, Alice had to struggle to carry on and care for Clatie and John no matter how deeply she felt her loss. Clatie recalls those difficult times:

My mother had two sisters. One was married and her husband was also in the Army Air Force. . . . My mother and her sister were living in a big house until my uncle got back and they kicked my mother out of the house. . . . She always said she was kicked out. . . . She didn't want to go. She begged not to go. . . . She moved to the house next door and it was improperly heated and that's when she got sick. She got pneumonia and then asthma, and they recommended that she either go to Arizona or Florida. We moved down to Florida in 1947. She had no family. She had no support. Everything was in New Jersey. She was totally alone with two children. . . . So really the connections died. Mother was on her own.

The memory of his father and the final price extracted from the family upon his loss remains an essential part of Clatie today. He admits to being confused by the events of his life, and his words are sometimes rambling:

My parents were in love. That marriage, it didn't die. We learned life after death. What we learned is that our father is here. This is what he wants us to do. A ghost figure—honor, duty and country. That's the way I was brought up.

At fifty I'm confused. Sometimes I ask why did my father die for this country. . . . What did we get? Forty-seven dollars a month. It's a contradiction, . . . he died for his country, but we don't want to be reminded that this happened. We were left and nobody knows how many orphans were left. This is what goes on in the United States. Well, somebody got killed; forget about it. In the United States we don't accept responsibility any more. It just blows my mind.

As children we never talked to others about it. Do you know how many people get really uptight when you say, "my father was killed in the war?" You're automatically shunned. It's like a sin. . . . They can't deal with it. . . . Theirs was a victory party. How are you going to party when all you're doing is basically sad?

My mother remarried after seven years. She wanted another ideal marriage, and it didn't work out that way. Our stepdad is also a veteran, but he didn't have the kind of manly quality that she was desiring. He didn't want to take responsibility. . . . She had the feeling of being a two-time loser. . . . He didn't take responsibility, the second one. Your ideal person, my father, went off to war. He was going to be a doctor when he got back. He was the football hero in high school, had all the ideal qualities, and he dies. We needed a father type, but he wasn't there. That was lack of support. We needed a father figure and then, our mother was our only guide. Even as guys, because we only had a mother, you have a tendency to view a woman differently. I feel like we picked up a lot of emotion which women feel. We identified with her. And of course, she needed us.

For me growing up without my father, I didn't feel whole, because I was missing a part. I was too young to understand if the people who knew him ever came to see us. When I realized what I could have done to find out about him, it was too late.

The ghost is there. My father did his honor thing. He didn't have to go. You know how it is to hear that? My father could have kept out of combat. Look what he put on the line. . . . There's no closure. . . . I can understand why other people would say, "Come on. Get on with your life." It's not that easy. It's my nature now. He's my hero, and I want to believe he died for something.

For Clatie, the loss of his "hero" was exacerbated by events of January 1982. While a member of the Army reserves, he helped recover bodies from the frigid waters of the Potomac River following the crash of Air Florida flight #90. His action earned him the Army Commendation Medal. It also served as an inevitable reminder of his own father's death in the waters of the South China Sea:

I spent ten days on active duty, clearing what was left of Air Florida, picking up bodies, transporting bodies, in cold weather, extreme weather, in the water. So I know a pair of gloves will shrink. . . . I was with two boats, and I do not wish to relate what I've seen.

The incident left Clatie with post-traumatic stress disorder. More recently, Clatie has been able to attach additional substance to the memory of his father. In 1987, he located a member of his father's crew, Lyle D. Kowalske, who had not flown on that mission of July 23, 1945. In a letter of July 29, Kowalske recalled Clatie's father:

The average mission was sixteen hours with one being eighteen hours. That was to Java. Most of the flights originated at night and usually two planes traveled together. If we didn't catch any shipping at night we'd bomb an airport or docks.

In spite of the low casualty rate, it was a very risky business, bad weather, uncharted mountains and B-24s had a habit of catching fire.

Because your dad was married, he never went to town with the boys, but he fit in good with the rest and he really knew his job.

As we were all nineteen and he was twenty-three, he was the one everyone went to with their problems.

He would light his pipe and keep us entertained with all of the incidents that happened to him in the Air Force. Did you know that for awhile he worked for the Ferry Command and flew B-17s across the Atlantic? Or that he went to glider school and was ready to graduate with a Warrant Officer rating, when they discontinued the program.

The one thing that air crew had was togetherness—they ate together, roomed together and did everything together. If you picked on one, you had to take on the whole crew. Fortunately we never had that problem. In a year's time, you can build up a close relationship and the loss of these brothers stays with you your whole life.

Not a day goes by that I don't think of them and say a prayer for them, even after all these years.

John, Clatie's twin, expresses a somewhat conflicting outlook on life as a war orphan. A number of his feelings—such as those concerning his stepfather—are not those of his brother's. At times, their differing childhood memories and adult perspectives are quite stark. Their contrasting view of the past serves as a reminder that quick and facile generalizations concerning the war orphan experience may be misleading or inaccurate:

My mother was very explicit, she kept all her records and everything. She has every letter, and every piece of paper that literally ever came in about my father. All the veteran's papers and everything.

It must have been when I was very young that I was told about my dad. From day one. As far back as I can remember. He was very articulate, very intelligent. My mother said he wanted to be a doctor. That's why he went into the service because there was a depression and all. You needed to have a way.

Dad came from Tennessee. A little bit hillbilly, but very sweet. Chattanooga is where he was raised. Harriman is where he was born. It is north of Chattanooga and off to the east. They were Irish. My grandfather was injured in World War I so he wasn't able to do too much. He did work some but it was smaller jobs. He was wounded four or five times.

Dad went right into the military after high school. Mom and Dad met in New Jersey. She went with a friend to a church or social club and they met there. You know how you go out with girl friends? It was some kind of social. My mother was Catholic, my father was Protestant. My mom's family was from Belleville, New Jersey. Her maiden name was Papartis and they were Lithuanian. Her father was a carpenter and furniture maker.

I feel I had a nice raising. I always knew about my father. My mother had the photo albums, she had all of his letters and she would read them to us. So I was very familiar with him in the sense of his writing and her recollections. I thought it was pretty normal. At school there wasn't much about being a war orphan. Very rarely did it come up. I can't really remember it ever coming up. My friends knew I had a stepfather and that my father was killed in World War II. But we never talked about it.

I was more of an introvert and Clatie, my twin brother, was more of an extrovert. Twins usually have one which is one, and one which is the other. He liked to go to the bowling alley and liked to go out more. He had a lot of friends. I went out a little bit to the bowling alley, I have a few trophies, we were on a few teams together. But I mostly stayed home and watched TV and read.

We had perhaps a little less money than some of the others. But my stepfather made a pretty good living. He worked and made a good salary at Cape Kennedy, so we were never really poor. He spent most of his years away from home over at Cape Kennedy and we would see him on the weekends. This month he will celebrate his forty-third year over there. We had a nice relationship. He commuted back and forth but we went on picnics and did the childhood stuff that all families do. It was a struggle to a point, because we weren't rich, but I think it was a middle-class existence.

My mother made happiness. I was happier when she was alive than any time in my life. My mother, if someone was down, could make you feel up. She had this way of bringing sunshine out of adversity. I can't explain how she did it, it was just something about her personality. Even her friends said that. If they were down or something she had a way of bringing them up. My mother's friends used to call her "Sunshine."

I think that had a lot to do with my not feeling down. My mother had a way of bringing out the best. She could make you feel better even when you were sad. She saved everything, all my father's records, all his medals, all his photos and she put everything in photo albums where you could see them, very easily obtainable.

She talked about my dad a lot. Just like if you were talking about a relative you wanted your kids to know about. She was sad about his death, but not about his life. Because he was a very nice man. She would have loved for him to be alive. She never made any bones about that, and that she would have had a very nice life if he had lived. So she was never in that sense sad, but she was sad he died.

She always wondered what kind of life she would have had. She had a lot of plans; they were going to buy a home and live in New Jersey. She had even thought about the plans for the house and they were going to buy a car. You know, the type of things people in the forties who had been through the depression would think about. She read to us a lot. In the beginning of course there was the childhood stuff, then she would explain the books and their philosophy behind them. She had a high school education. Getting an education was one of her principles. In those days just graduating from high school was important and of course she brought that value to us. She wanted to make sure we were educated.

I finished two years of college but after that I didn't have enough money to continue because I would have to go upstate. I got the GI Bill but I only received $77 a month. So I had to live at home and go to school. In order to finish my education I would have had to go away and I did not have the money to do that.

My father left the insurance money to my mother and his mother. My mother got half. My father also put his mother on the insurance. It made money tight. That was something he chose, so what were you going to do? My mother never discussed it very much.

My father's mother came to see us when we were growing up but not the brothers. They were also very young. Two were in the military and one was still in high school when my father died. He was the eldest. They stayed in the military and after they got out they wanted to socialize with us more. They are nice men. But I have very little memory of them in my youth. Now my grandmother Cunningham wrote letters and sent presents. She came for visits. When we sent her photos she would have to mark the photos on the back saying which was Clatie, the grandson, because Clatie as a young boy looked almost identical to my father. So in order not to mix the photos up she would mark them on the back who was who. My mother always told Clatie he looked like our dad.

I was very proud of my dad. Every time we have Memorial Day, and things like that, I am very proud my father served. Of course you are always sad he died, I can't deny that. But I am still glad he served. I have always wondered how it would be to talk to him. I have a pretty good idea though, because my mother would relate things to us.

All of his uniforms were tailor-made. That is how particular he was. He wouldn't use the ones that were issued by the government. He would take them and have them altered by a tailor. His hair had to be exactly right. He was very articulate. My mother liked him very much. He had a beautiful southern accent. Because he was from Chattanooga he had that southern drawl. Mother said you could cut it with a knife.

In those days all Mother's friends and relatives always said that my mother was a very happy person. She tried to make other people happy. She realized they were living in a depression but she believed you had to look towards the positive, that someday it was going to get better. That kind of happiness is what I am referring to. She looked for the best. In other words, the cup is half full, not half empty.

She put us kids number one. She always made sure our home-work was done; she always made sure we got home safe from school. She walked to school and walked my sister home to make sure she was safe, with the traffic and everything. My mother was always very careful with the children to make sure everything was safe. She just wanted to make sure that nothing went wrong. She invested a lot of time and effort in her kids and she wanted to make sure everything was positive with them, that everything came out right.

When we were very young Mom liked to dress Clatie and me the same. We dressed alike almost to the sixth grade. After that we started dressing differently. She would mark each shirt, because there were identical shirts, one with two dots for me, one dot for Clatie. Everything we owned we would know exactly which pair of socks were ours, and everything. He had a dresser drawer and I had one, and even though we wore the exact same clothes she knew exactly which pair of everything belonged to who.

I didn't mind wearing the same clothes. Clatie I think minded it a little bit, especially as he got older. But I didn't mind it at all. I love being a twin. To me it is something special. We had teachers that would write in the book that we were like Tweedledum and Tweedledee. We matched each other. But I was an introvert and he was an extrovert. Almost like salt and pepper shakers. A matched set, a set of book ends or something. People liked that. I could almost read Clatie's mind and he could almost read mine, we were that close. We knew what each other would want out of a situation. Up until the fifth grade we had the same teacher.

My mother's family was supportive. My grandmother would write once or twice a week when she was alive. Mother knew everything that was going on up North because every day she would go to the mail box and get a letter from my grandmother or aunts. In those days people loved to write so you would get a lot of letters. Now it's the telephone. She didn't like living so far away but my grandmother wanted to move to Florida. They owned vacant lots next to each other. Grandmother only came to visit, though, she didn't come to live. But my mother had asthma so bad she couldn't work. So bad that is was tough just taking care of her kids. She was never very healthy. Even though she was not feeling well though, she always got up. She would push herself.

I remember moving in with my stepfather, even though I was young. I liked him. I liked him very much. We would go swimming and picnicking, that kind of stuff. I didn't know if it was different than any other reality.

I worked for a retail store in Tampa, and retired after twenty years. I was the mail room supervisor. I never dealt with too many people. I never had a large circle of friends or anything like that. It may have been because of what happened. You never know. It was just my life and you live it. Like I said, I was an introvert anyway. When you're an introvert it doesn't bother you as much as it would if you were an extrovert. I never married; I don't know why but I really don't deal that much with people. I am more of a homebody. I don't go out to clubs because I don't drink. I garden a little. I just bought a new home and put in flowers and stuff. My sister and I live together and own it together.

I think being a war orphan had a few down effects. But when I was in school I don't remember it was mentioned. I would, of course, have loved to have had my father and would have loved to have him survive. But I think when you are being raised in a certain way, that is the universe you live in, it is your reality. As you get older, and you can look back then you can relate it to other peoples' lives. But when you are actually living it, it is hard to know because it is your reality at the time. I think I would have been different if my father lived. He would have been more of a driver. There would have been two drivers instead of just one, my mom. When you have two people, you get better grades and stuff. But at the time I was living it, that was my life.

When Mother first moved to Florida it was very hard for her. She was twenty-six years old. She was twenty-three years old when Dad was killed. But she met my stepdad within a short time. My mother was at the beach with relatives and met my stepfather. I think she loved my stepdad. She died of a heart attack at age sixty-seven years old. That affected me quite a lot, very, very much. It seems to affect you for the rest of your life. We were very close as people are when there are very few people around.

Her death was very hard. My stepfather aged quite a bit from it, you can see it physically. He is not the type of man that shows a lot of emotion but you can see it in his physical being. His hair got extremely grey, and his face got older than his age very quickly. He is not the kind of man to express it in words but you can see it in his actual being, in his face.

Clatie may have been more affected by our father's death because he is more outgoing. I was more conservative. I only had but five long-term friends. But between not having relatives, and not having friends I am able to enjoy my life with less people around. I think Clatie liked to be around people. He likes to be around people more constantly. He probably wanted more out of life than maybe he got.[1]

[1]Susan Hadler's interview with Clatie Cunningham III on October 21, 1995; Ann Mix's interview with John Cunningham on March 21, 1997; letter from Alice to Ray, July 12, 1945; letter from Lyle D. Kowalske, July 29, 1987; AWON files.

Alice S. Papartis and S/Sgt. Clatie R. Cunningham, Jr., 9 February 1944.

(l-r) Clatie, Alice and John Cunningham, circa 1947 in Tampa, Florida.

Back row, l-r: Clatie R. Cunningham, Nicholas Meriage, A. S. Pitt, John W. Knigga, Charles E. Carroll, Lyle D. Kowalske, Roy E. Hayes. Front row, l-r: Ed Gingrich, Walter N. Low, Don McDermott, Stanley L. Reed. Photo taken 9 January 1945 of the 868th Bombardment Squadron.

Sam:
My Father's Dead and My Mother's Crazy

$\mathcal{S}$am grew up in the Williamsburg section of Brooklyn. "Even then," he recalls, "it was a slum." His mother Bertha (he never called her mom) was psychotic, the seeds of which Sam believed went back to her own childhood:

Her father died when she was sixteen. He became ill when she was twelve. At that time, she was expected partially to replace him before and after school, selling bananas from a pushcart. In those days, bananas were sold four for a nickel. Her three brothers also stood in the snow and the sweltering heat, but because she was the only girl, she was also the assistant cook and maid for "the boys."

There was also the death of her mother. I really don't remember my maternal grandmother. The few pictures I have seem to show her as a harsh woman, but maybe that's because she had a harsh life. I don't know what Bertha's relationship with her mother was like. We lived nearby but not with my grandmother. I do remember

113

my mother cried at my grandmother's funeral. It was the only time I ever saw her cry. Scream—always; cry—once.

Last, there was the loss of her job. She was trained as a book-keeper, proud to be a high school graduate and claimed to have had a piano recital at Carnegie Hall and broke her collarbone while play-ing handball. Why did this renaissance woman lose her job? I don't know. We never spoke about it. We never spoke about many things. She was busy communicating with and about my dead father.

Henry I. Tannenbaum, the man with whom Bertha "communicated," had been in the 331st Infantry Regiment, 83rd Division. He died outside the small Belgium village of Ottre on January 11, 1945, during the Battle of the Bulge. Sam's mother never accepted the death of Henry (as in the case of Bertha, Sam always referred to his father by his first name). In-stead, she believed that he was communicating with her by means of the apartment's radio, and that he would return to his wife and son when his secret government mission was over:

Bertha had developed a unique mythology about my father. It involved a radio without a cabinet. Bertha would get telepathic messages from the radio. It did not matter if the radio was on or off. The radio would tell her that Henry was working as an undercover agent for the FBI. As soon as he finished his current case, he would return to us and take us out of the slum we called home. The prob-lem was that he kept getting new cases.

Bertha's psychotic behavior ultimately went beyond communicating with a dead husband:

I guess I knew she was "different" the night she attempted her suicide and my murder. I was eight years old. The doctors called that her first psychotic episode. She sealed the windows with tow-els, turned on the gas oven, blew out the pilot light and ordered me to sleep. After she was asleep, I got up, turned off the oven and opened the windows.

The immediate trigger of her psychotic episode was a man who exposed himself to her while she was walking in the street. She was upset by her powerlessness and decided to kill herself and me as well. She rarely left our apartment again, except for her second psychotic episode, a series of bizarre events that cost her thousands of dollars, and her final psychotic episode when she was evicted from her apartment and sent to Pilgrim State Hospital in Brentwood, New York.

Sam recalled the conditions of his childhood in Williamsburg:

So at age eight, my father was dead, my mother tried to kill herself and murder me, her parents were dead, and I had no contact with my father's family. After the death of her mother, Bertha's immediate family consisted of her three brothers and their wives and children. I had little contact with most of them while I was growing up. Ironically I am closer with them now, but as a child I did not have much of a support system.

That's how we lived for many years: Bertha screamed at her husband, the FBI agent, to come home; I shopped, cooked, did the laundry, and went to school.

School was okay until the fourth grade. I hated my fourth grade teacher. She was an incompetent. . . . Back then I was a truant, so they sent a truant officer to my home, and Bertha refused to talk to him, so I kept on "playing hookey." On Thanksgiving eve, the vice principal came into my class and asked what I was thankful for. I said, "Nothing." He said, "Aren't you thankful for your parents?" I said, "No, my father's dead and my mother's crazy." My classmates loved it. They didn't know any other half-orphans, but crazy is funny in the fourth grade, and they loved the anti-authoritarianism.

That wisecrack probably saved my life. I was transferred to another class, where the teacher asked me about Bertha. I told her about the constant screaming. She suggested I stop feeling sorry for myself (get off your high horse) and that I spend my time at the public library, doing homework and reading books. I did.

My grades soared, and I had a "normal" life. I would eat a big breakfast (still do), go to school, go to the library until closing time, and go home. If Bertha were asleep, I was safe. If not, I would stuff cotton in my ears until the screaming died down.

How did I eat, buy necessities, sign report cards, all that normal stuff? Easy. Bertha would get a government allotment check based on my father's death. She did not acknowledge his death, but she let me sign her name and cash her check. . . . I paid for groceries, clothes, shoes, and utilities by cash and even managed to save some money. How could a banker let an eight-year-old cash a check? Simple. I went to a bank teller who lived in the building and heard my mother's screams. So what? Everybody screamed. Some did it in Spanish, Italian, Greek, and Polish. Bertha happened to scream in English and Yiddish. We were just a loud international building. The teller would cash Bertha's check for me and keep a little something for herself. Was she an opportunist? Absolutely. But she helped me and she taught me the art of compromise. If you want to get a little, you've got to give a little.

Although his father's relatives lived quite close, Sam had no contact with them because of family differences:

Why, you might ask, did I not know my father's family when his younger sister lived about two miles away? Well, Bertha didn't talk to my father's family after she received the little yellow telegram. "The Secretary of War desires me to express his deep regret that your husband private Henry I. Tannenbaum was killed in action on eleven January in Belgium. Further report states he had returned to duty twelve December from previously reported wound. Confirming letter follows. The Adjitant [sic] General." Today there is personal contact and counseling for the widow. Then there was just a misspelled telegram.

The estrangement was because Bertha wanted the body to stay in Belgium. They wanted Henry to be buried in a family plot. They won. She never talked to or about them again. I never saw my father's grave, about a twenty-minute ride from my house, until I was thirteen.

Bertha's second psychotic episode came when Sam was thirteen. She decided to give Sam a bar mitzvah party. Despite the ongoing estrangement, the invitations would include her husband's family:

Bertha bought clothes for herself and presents for both families. We're talking fur coats, movie cameras, and expensive jewelry. My mother's family returned most of their presents, my father's family accepted them. Nobody asked why. I estimate she spent over $10,000. Where did she get the money? I think it was in a trust fund set up from either her father's estate or my father's insurance policy. Why didn't she use that money to get us out of the slums? My guess is because she was waiting for Henry to take us out. Why did she give strangers money? Simple. It was in appreciation of my father's imminent homecoming. Well, he never came home. When she ran out of money, she borrowed about $500 from my bar mitzvah gifts to pay bills. The only written acknowledgment of her behavior for all those years revolves around that $500. She wrote in my junior-high school autograph book, "I lost the $500 bet." What that meant was she bet me my father was coming home and she lost.

After the bar mitzvah, I had minimal contact with my father's family with one notable exception. When my paternal grandfather died, I went to his funeral alone, because Bertha was back to being a recluse. At the funeral, someone asked for pall bearers and shouted the name "Sam." They meant a nephew of my grandfather, but I stepped forward and lifted the coffin, the youngest pall bearer and the only grandchild. I didn't see them again until I invited them to my first wedding, about twelve years later.

Sam did have some support from his mother's youngest brother, Uncle Sid, in facing various mini-crises with Bertha:

Life with Bertha was "normal." She shouted, I studied. I skipped a year in school and made the National Honor Society. . . . I did have help from my Uncle Sidney, my mother's youngest brother, when Bertha had a mini-psychotic episode (she bit my arm and ordered me out of the house). I stayed with Sid and Hilda for about two weeks, but they lived in Queens near the Nassau County border (really the suburbs then), and I was a city kid. Bertha calmed down (stopped screaming after midnight) and I moved back in.

Sam graduated from high school when he was sixteen years old and found a job that summer working on the docks unloading ships:

I worked that summer as a longshoreman unloading sugar from Cuba (this was pre-Castro). The work was hot, dirty, and dangerous, but it paid well. . . . I grossed $600 on Labor Day weekend. Then I discovered the wonderful world of tax deductions and vowed never to work that hard for so little money, ever again.

The $600 went to pay medical bills when I had my appendix removed. Bertha could not afford any medical insurance, and we never applied for any kind of welfare. Coming home from the hospital was an experience. I could not walk up four flights of stairs, so I got four friends to carry me up on a chair. They were excited since they had never seen my apartment. I was concerned that they would drop me when Bertha started to scream at Henry. She did not scream. Instead, she hid in the bathroom. They left; I recovered and went off to college.

For Sam, there remained the challenge of devising a way to pay for college:

Brooklyn College in those days was tuition free, but I couldn't live at home, so I got a day job and went to college at night. I calculated that it would take forever to graduate, so I decided to take advantage of the war orphan scholarship and use that money to pay for my living expenses while I went to college in the daytime.

Rent for a furnished apartment with a hot plate was $65 a month so I knew I could swing it. I asked my mother to sign the application. She refused. Her logical reason? Henry was alive; therefore, I wasn't a war orphan; and, therefore, I wasn't entitled to a war orphan scholarship.

So I convinced Uncle Sid that he could be my guardian just for the purpose of applying. I spoke to a lawyer, cousin George, and asked him to be prepared to draw up guardianship papers if the bureaucrats gave me a hard time. I brought my father's death certificate, my birth certificate, my uncle, and my mother's telephone number. I asked the bureaucrat to ask my mother over the phone to sign the application. He did. She apparently told him that he was involved in some FBI plot with my father and that she would not cooperate. [Ultimately, I worked it out and] I received a full four-year scholarship to a tuition free college.

When Sam married, Bertha refused to attend:

My Aunt Molly, widow of my mother's middle brother Jack, went to my mother's house and begged her to come to my wedding. Bertha refused, believing it to be another FBI plot. . . . Later I got divorced, moved out of New York City, and told Bertha, I'd see her when I could. My ex-wife promised to take my daughter Lisa to see her, and they did. I got engaged and my fiancée, now wife of ten years, Rachel, wanted to meet Bertha. I flew [Bertha] down to Florida. Rachel loved Bertha, Bertha loved Rachel. They cooked together, Bertha for the first time in years. This wedding she comes to. She wears a wig, I don't know why. True to form, Bertha told Rachel that the time is right and that Henry will be here soon. Officially he's been dead thirty-six years at that point.

Looking back on his life, Sam concludes:

So what was it like growing up as a Jewish war orphan in Williamsburg, Brooklyn, New York? It was a life like any other life, filled with pain and pleasure. Henry gave me intelligence (he was a Latin and Greek scholar) and according to Aunt Molly he also gave me my sense of humor. Bertha gave me an appreciation of the finer things in life (during her brief spending spree we went to operas and museums) and an abiding respect for all human beings, no matter how powerless.

Today, my lifestyle has what some might consider contradictory aspects. I read the *Wall Street Journal* and the *National Enquirer*. I listen to classical and country music. I attend ballets and watch pro wrestling. I play racquet ball and bowl. I am at times selfish, at other times generous.

I didn't expect any special treatment because my father was killed in World War II. I didn't expect any special treatment because my mother was mentally ill. I learned early on that life is hard. I worked hard in school. I worked hard at work. My work as a fund-raising consultant brings me in contact with the rich and powerful. I treat them all with respect as I hope they would treat me. I am not impressed by their wealth, only by their actions on behalf of those less fortunate. I work hard at play. I work hard at being a good husband and father.

My personal philosophy? Don't complain, don't explain, just do it. I try to create solutions, not problems. I live my life trying to anticipate others' needs. I figure if I meet their needs, someday they will meet mine. Most of the time, it works.

Although Sam has achieved success as an adult, the scars from his war orphan status remain close to the surface. In a letter to Ann Mix in December 1991, he noted:

As I told you on the phone, this (whatever this is) is very difficult for me emotionally, so I will respond as though AWON was just another organization needing my help. Rest assured it is not, but that is the best way for me to deal with it now. . . . Right now I can't get through the AWON brochure without crying.[1]

[1]Statement by Samuel V. Tannenbaum, December 1991; letter from Samuel V. Tannenbaum to Ann Mix, December 17, 1991; AWON files.

(l–r) Samuel Victor Tannenbaum, Bertha Fidel Tannenbaum, Private Henry Irving Tannenbaum in July 1944 at Livingston Manor, New York.

"'White Death' is the title of the last known photograph of my father, taken by Tony Vaccaro. My father is face down in the snow near the Belgium village of Ottre. The photo was taken on January 11, 1945, during the Battle of the Bulge. The subtitle reads, 'Requiem for a dead soldier. Private Henry I. Tannenbaum. Tannenbaum signifies an evergreen tree; it is the time of year when his name evokes images of snow and Christmas.'" Photo courtesy Tony Vaccaro.

★
★
★
★
★
★ John:
★ *The Hurt Never Goes Away*
★

★

★

★ ***J***ohn was three months old when his Army father Frank Dell died. In
1990, reacting to an article in *Parade* magazine concerning American orphans of the Vietnam War, John wrote these two letters. The first letter
went to Friends of the Vietnam Veterans Memorial:

May 27, 1990

I'm gonna preface this by saying that I never write letters like
this to anybody. But after reading the article in today's *Parade* about
the experiences of you and other people who had lost their dads in
war, I felt I had to tell you why this hits home.

Like you, I never knew my dad. He was killed in the South
Pacific during World War II when I was three months old. At age
forty-six, I guess I'm old enough to be *your* father.

And let me tell you one thing: the feeling of—what? loss? grief?
being gypped—*never* goes away. I guess what I'm saying is that for
something of this magnitude, it doesn't matter if you're six years
old, or ten or eighteen or thirty one or forty six or probably seventy.

I think what you and this organization are doing is terrific. No one knows better than myself what it's like to be the only kid on the block who didn't have a dad.

I'm gonna lay some things on you that you may or may not be familiar with. My guess is that you'll know instantly what I'm talking about, though.

—It's "father-and-son night" at your elementary school. Instead of going (because obviously you *can't*) you stay home, go to bed at 7:30 and cry your guts out into the pillow, hoping your mom won't hear because you really don't feel like talking about it.

—You're six years old and you're at a park on one of those hand-push merry-go-round things and someone else's dad is pushing you. As he's giving this thing a shove, his arm goes across your shoulder, and you realize that this is the first time in your life that a dad has come in any physical contact with you. (I'm sorry, but six-year-olds just shouldn't ever have to think in these terms.)

—It's an *embarrassment* when anyone asks you where your dad is. When this happens you just want to go somewhere and die, because you're "different."

—For want of something better to do one day, you just start saying the word "dad," and realize how totally alien it sounds.

—You feel a horrendous mistake has been made somewhere. Why are *you* the only kid in the world without a father? Yeah, sure, along the line you meet other kids whose dads have died, but at least they *knew* their fathers—if only for a few years.

Now maybe you were one of the lucky ones and your mom remarried. I wasn't, because mine didn't. Hence, in my case, I didn't even have a *stepdad*.

I say this because I hope you had the semblance of a normal "Ozzie & Harriet" type of family life *despite* the fact your real dad wasn't around to share it.

The one thing that particularly blew me out of the water in the *Parade* article was how you recounted fantasies of your dad walking up to you on the practice field and saying, "Hi, I'm your dad." This is *exactly* the fantasy that I had thirty years ago. Despite the facts of the situation, I always had it in the back of my mind that there was a *slight* chance that someone had fucked up somewhere and my dad was just gonna come strollin' into my life, albeit a decade or so later.

For some reason, the situation hit me with a vengeance when I was in high school. I went out and bought a bunch of WWII-era records, such as "Praise the Lord and Pass the Ammunition," "Goodbye, Mama, I'm Off to Yokohama" and my own personal favorite, "Lili Marlene." I'd lock myself in my room with a couple of bottles of RC Cola, and listen to these records over and over and over again, *knowing* that my dad had known them. I guess this was my grieving period—when, for the first time in my life, I really truly realized that Frank Dell was not going to come back, not ever, *ever.*

Unfortunately, I didn't even have any *pictures* of my dad, since they'd gotten lost along with a bunch of other stuff by Bekins when we moved across town when I was three-years old. To compound the situation, my mom and dad had only known each other a few months before they got married. He'd apparently pissed off his family somewhere along the line, and he'd never discussed his family with my mom. Neither I nor my mom even know if I had grandparents, aunts, uncles, etc., somewhere. (The fact that my dad was from New York City didn't help much. You ever try to track down someone with a relatively common name who came from New York City?)

However, being of the school that says, "Okay, it's fine to be pissed off about what might have been—but let's just get on with our life"—I did precisely that.

To compensate for the lack of a father figure, I went into law enforcement right after I got out of the Air Force. Being a cop took me into the realm of "guys," and I really got off on it.

After nearly twenty years with my department, however, I got bored and became a paralegal in a law office. I'm going to law school at night, and in a couple of years should be a practicing attorney, if all goes well.

I can honestly tell you that there isn't a day that goes by that I don't think of my dad. And I never even *knew* him.

And even now, forty-six years after he was killed, his "being" will occasionally come flooding back to me.

F'rinstance: A couple of weeks ago, my mom was prowling around her garage for something and found this long-forgotten box full of crap. In it was a love note to her from my dad—the only tangible proof of his existence that I'd ever seen. I was stunned. The handwriting was exactly—and I mean *exactly*—like mine. I'm going to tell you the following, however, in hope that you will understand what I'm saying, and will hopefully spread the message to your compadres in your organization:

Okay. You know how they say that in every cloud there's a silver lining? Well, the silver lining in my case is that I, myself, am the best damned father in the world.

I have two sons, who are age seventeen and nineteen. They are both model children. Both are straight-A students (one in high school and one at UC-Santa Barbara.) They have no hang-ups, neuroses, major problems, or psychoses. They don't smoke, drink or do drugs. They're happy, well-adjusted boys, who will come to me or their mom with their problems, without fear of repercussion or put-down. We can (and do) discuss everything. (And I mean *everything*.)

To put this in even better perspective, I have had *school counselors* ask me and my wife what our secret of parenting is, because our kids are just so damn decent.

Now, perhaps if I'd had a dad, I wouldn't have put that much effort into raising kids on my own. Perhaps if I'd had a dad, I would have thought that parenting was just parenting. But as it is, I have a *respect* for what it's like to be a dad myself.

Good luck in your efforts, guy. As one who lived through this a long, long time ago (and who is *still living* through it) I hope and pray that you and your contemporaries find the solace that you need. If there had been a group like yours around when I was going through this, I wouldn't have felt so all alone and so left out.

As I write this, it's Memorial Day Eve. Even though I'm not what you might consider religious, when I go to bed tonight I'm going to say a little prayer. And it's going to be something like this:

God, please make sure that our guys who were killed in combat know that we appreciate what they did for us. You took my dad. I don't know why *him*, but there must have been a reason. And because of my dad and guys like him, I live in a country in which I can say anything I damn well please: and I can do anything reasonable I want to and not have to fear repercussion.

Thank you also for giving me the strength to make a man out of myself, all *by* myself, even though I didn't have a dad to help me in the process.

Hang in there guy. It's an agony, and it'll always *be* an agony. What you're doing is wonderful. God, how I wish something like this had existed for us WWII "half-orphans."

Why hasn't someone been aware of this *before*?

Sincerely yours,

John

The second letter, written a few months later, went to Ann Mix and AWON:

September 17, 1990

You were referred to me by *Parade* magazine.

See, in May, *Parade* magazine ran this absolutely incredible article about "orphans" of the Vietnam conflict. I felt called upon to respond, as my dad was a World War II casualty, and I never knew him.

Today, *Parade* replied to my letter, and gave me your name and address, and an article outlining what you're doing.

I'm *enclosing* a copy of the letter I wrote to the Friends of the Vietnam Veterans Memorial (subject of the *Parade* article), as I think it's pretty self-explanatory. (Translate that to, I wrote this down once, and I'm afraid that's all I'm good for, as I really can't go through it again.)

In November, I'll be forty-seven. The hurt never goes away, nor does the stigma of being "different" because you don't have a dad. While I've "risen above it" and it certainly doesn't rule my life, the fact remains that to this day I feel gypped out of a normal life and upbringing. While I don't dwell on it, it's always in the back of my mind that I *am* different from most people, and that had I not been a strong person, I might *really* have been fucked up.

I think a book detailing World War II "orphans" is terrific. While I think my experience is unique (a mother who never even considered dating, hence a *totally* male-less atmosphere) I think it's safe to say that I'm in the same boat with you: A kid whose life was drastically altered by a horrible quirk of fate.

My message to Frank Dell, if he could hear me?

Hey, dad. I think you did okay. You've got a son who turned out alright, and a couple of grandkids you'd really be proud of. It would've been nice to have known you, but I understand. Truly, I do. But I *am* pissed at government red tape, and I *am* leaning kind of toward the agnostic side, because what God in His right mind would play such serious mind-fuck with a little kid, as was played with me?

But, hey, life goes on, eh?

Well, at least for *some* of us, it does. It didn't for you, and for that I'll always be resentful.

Anyhow, I'm sorry if I got a little carried away. Please understand one thing: This is a topic I don't even discuss with my wife.

Other than this, however, I'm really a very normal, average guy.

It still hurts, though.

Very truly yours,

John [1]

[1]Emphasis in the original letters of May 27, 1990, and September 17, 1990; letters in AWON files.

Nancy:
Yes, I Am Your Daughter

*C*aptain Andrew W. Rougvie of the Army Air Force graduated from Brown University, Class of 1933. A native of Providence, Rhode Island, he had enlisted in the military in June 1942. After duty in the United States, the Army Air Force sent him to China in November 1943; he died there on July 17, 1945. The end of the fighting lay less than a month away.

Captain Rougvie's daughter, Nancy, had already passed her twelfth birthday. She had strong memories of her father, a fact that made an important difference in her life:

Being a bit older than most World War II orphans, I have some wonderful memories of my dad. I was twelve-and-a-half years old when he died, and ten when I last spent time with him. He died just two days after his thirty-fourth birthday, which I thought was ancient at the time but now realize just how young he was.

In a letter to the AWON, Nancy recalled the news of her father's loss, including the fact that his letters from China continued to arrive after the notification of his death:

The telegram arrived in the morning; we received letters from him the same afternoon! There was always a bit of unreality about it all. For years I watched the newsreels of returning servicemen looking for his face in the crowd. Until I received your literature, I thought I was the only one with such reactions.

The existence of a healthy and close-knit family provided stability and love for Nancy:

Mother and I lived with Daddy's parents from about the time he enlisted until a year after his death, so we were extremely fortunate to have a very strong family, and it gave me male role models par excellence. Not only did I have the greatest grandfather in the world, but a great-uncle, and two uncles. We have always been a close family and remain so now—even though we aren't many in number. Mother was originally from Maine—her mother had died when Mother was only three and her father had died just three days after my parents eloped, so her life had not been easy. Daddy's family became hers.

The body of Nancy's father was brought back to Arlington Cemetery, and she attended the ceremony:

The decision was made to have Daddy's remains returned to Arlington. At that time, there was no national cemetery in Rhode Island and my grandfather Morrill was buried at Arlington, so it was Mother's choice. Her father had served in the Spanish-American War, the Mexican Uprising [the 1916 incursion into Mexico against Pancho Villa], the Philippine Insurrection, and World War I. I have lovely photos of the service held in Kunming [China]. Later we learned Daddy's remains had been transferred to the Punch Bowl Cemetery and, on November 12, 1947, he was finally laid to rest at Arlington. We were fortunate to be able to attend the service. Many [orphans] could [not] or did not. It had not been until I started to think about what I might write that I realized I do not know another war orphan here in Rhode Island! I do not recall any of my close friends losing their father, although a couple were in service.

At the time of the dedication of our World War II Memorial here in Providence, I was privileged to be invited to sit on the platform for the ceremony. It had not been planned. They were looking for a Gold Star Mother and could not find one; my Uncle Bob yelled out, "How about a Gold Star Daughter," and there I was.

Nancy also has her father's letters and some books, another crucial link to her dad.

One of the many, many things I have always thought about doing—and with the computer it might just happen someday—is to transcribe Daddy's letters. He did not complain about adverse living conditions (except to say the mosquitoes would untie the netting in order to get to him), but he wrote about life in China, about the children. I still cannot read them easily—I dissolve in tears even after forty-seven years! All his letters to my mother are also preserved. . . . Daddy was about to be transferred and had packed up about seven crates of books to establish a library there in China, but they all came back to us; most were donated to a state library here in Providence. Some I still have and dearly treasure them.

Nancy summarized her thoughts about her father:

He was a wonderful person, and I've always been very proud to have been his daughter (because I'm an only child, he often called me his favorite son as I was a bit of a tomboy). He was a political science major and would probably have become involved in many of the same things I have become involved in. I have worked as a housing coordinator (landlord / tenant rights and responsibilities, apartment referrals, etc.) and am still quite involved in arson prevention. He had been a union organizer, and I agree with his principles and reasons for that day, yet I have never belonged to a union for many of the same reasons he was in favor of them. So I'm sure we would have been on opposite sides of some issues. One day when running up the steps of our Capitol when I was involved in some legislation, I heard myself saying, "Yes, I am your daughter!" The loss will always be there—how I wish I had known him as an adult.[1]

[1]Letters to Ann Mix, May 22, 1992, and August 9, 1992; clipping from the *Providence Journal Bulletin,* no date [July 1945?]; AWON files.

(l–r) Private Andrew W. Rougvie, Jr., Nancy Anne Rougvie, and David W. Rougvie (Andrew's older brother), during the spring of 1943 in Providence. Andrew's younger brother, Robert Francis Rougvie, was in the Air Corps.

Nancy Anne Rougvie and Andrew W. Rougvie, Jr., during the summer of 1934 in Providence, Rhode Island.

Andrew White Rougvie, Jr., Captain, U.S. Air Corps. Born 11 July 1911 in Providence, Rhode Island. Died 17 July 1945, Kunming, China.

John:

When I Had My Own Children. . . .
I Didn't Know What to Do

*M*ajor John Nichols, Sr., of the 106th Infantry Battalion, 27th Infantry Division, died in late June 1944, during the assault on Saipan. He had served in the Marines during the 1920s, seeing duty in the Far East, but had then left the service to return to upstate New York, not far from Utica. He did not leave military life entirely, however, for he joined the New York National Guard. When it was called into national service as the 27th Infantry Division in October 1940, John Nichols went with it. The Division became a veteran unit of the Pacific War, with combat on Makin, Saipan, and Okinawa.[1] That veteran status, however, came at a price, and John Nichols and his family paid part of it. His service earned him the Silver Star and the Bronze Star with Oak Leaf Clusters. He was forty-one years old when he died from a Japanese sniper's bullet.[2]

His son, John, Jr., was nine years old when the news arrived of his father's death. At the time, his mother worked at Remington Arms, while his maternal grandmother lived with them and helped watch over young John. Both his grandparents on his father's side had been deceased for some years. John was outside playing with friends when the notification arrived:

I was playing on the street, and a guy came and just knocked on the door. My grandmother answered it. He handed her a telegram and took off. . . . I can't blame the Western Union guy. My God, he was probably scared to death. . . . She opened the telegram and she started screaming. My mother hadn't come home from work yet. My grandmother hollered from the yard, "Come on home."

He remembers well his mother's reaction: "She just went out of it. I can remember it seemed like days that all she did was lay on the couch and cry." Although she later would date, she never remarried.

Later that year, an officer came to the house to complete the government's notification process:

It was probably three months later that this major comes by with my father's medals. He brought my father's Silver Star and Bronze Star and the Purple Heart and presented them to my mother. . . . There was a memorial service at my aunt's house because she had a bigger parlor, and there were other members of the family there. The thing took fifteen minutes, I guess. The major read a couple of things and made the presentation of the flag and the medals.

Being nine years old when his father died, John retains some memories of him:

He had a pipe stand, and he would come home from work and he would light up a pipe and smoke the pipe. He used to hang around mostly with his National Guard friends, where we would go on picnics and things like that. I remember parades. He belonged to a group—I've often wondered about it. They were called the Redmen and they would dress up like Indians, and they would participate in these parades. After the war, I never heard of them, anything about them. I don't know if it was a nationwide organization or if it was just something local. You know, whooping it up and dancing, that type of thing. They weren't marching like you would expect.

John also recalls his father's stern discipline that his boyhood misbehavior occasionally triggered:

Oh, he licked me a couple of times, I remember that. I deserved it. One of his friends was at our house. I was an only son, and they had an only daughter, and she was my age, and I never liked her. Something like Dennis the Menace and Margaret, I guess. Anyway, I heard that she [was afraid of the dark and] couldn't go to sleep without a light on. They were over visiting, and off our kitchen, under the stairs, there was a door and there was a storage place. Somehow I coaxed Linda [through the door] and I shut the door on her. She screamed and yelled, and I went right over his knee right then and there.

I remember another time, they were going somewhere, I guess on a Sunday or something, and I didn't want to go and I "ran away," and my older cousin captured me. At least my father didn't wait. He spanked me right there and said, "Get in the car."

With his father's death, his grandmother told him, "You're the man of the house now." Along with such household tasks as stoking the coal furnace and removing the ashes, John took jobs delivering papers and setting pins in a bowling alley. Then in high school he became first an usher and later an assistant manager at the town movie theater.

Hard work, however, could not lessen the loss of a father. Occasional events added to John's pain and bewilderment:

There was a guy across the street, an old guy. I guess he was retired. And as kids we used to play, like in the summer particularly, and run between the houses, and we would make noise. Anyway, he slept during the day and was up at night. I don't know if he had a part-time job or what, but he was an old grouch anyway. One day he was irritated. I ran through there and made some noise, and he made some comments about, "Glad your father got killed," or something like that. And that hurt. So from then on, every chance I had, I would run between the houses, so I got back at him.

And I remember one time, I guess it was a rainy night, I went to the factory to meet my mother at the exit, and this was just before the war ended. So it was near to my father getting killed. I was standing there waiting, and two guys came out and there was a whole ' crowd of people coming out, and there was a narrow doorway. I was just standing there holding an umbrella, and one guy said something to the fact that, "I hope this war never ends, we're making so much money." I had no idea who they were. They just stunned me.

John would particularly feel the loss of a male role model when it came time for him to become a father:

I think the thing is that when I had my own children—I have three sons—in those critical years, I really didn't know what to do for them when I was with them. [I had to] sort of watch what the others did.

Although there were plenty of children in the neighborhood with whom to play, John recalled that there was a missing element to his childhood games:

There was no one in the neighborhood who came forth and included me with their children or anything like that. They went on vacation or they went what-have-you, that was their thing, but I was never included with anybody else.

Ultimately, John would join the Marine Corps. Looking back on it, he feels it was meant to be. In the Corps, he found his home:

I was the sole surviving son, so I didn't have to go into the service, but everyone else did, and I felt it was in my blood, and I think it was. I did three years, and I was stationed in one place, Norfolk, and I hated it. I got out and went to the local college. Well, I arranged it so I had all morning classes and every afternoon I was in a local bar, raising hell, as young men do. And the recession of '58 hit, and I couldn't get a job back at [Remington] Arms for summer work. I needed that job to go back to school. And then the Lebanon crisis hit in the summer of '58. I said, "That's it. It's over." Three years on the day that I got out, I reenlisted, and since I had three years of college, about two years later, I applied for a commission. The Marine Corps had a short-fall from the colleges, a big short-fall, so they dipped into the ranks, and I got a commission. I had found a home.

John served two tours in Vietnam and retired from the Marines as a major, the same rank his father had held. Ironically for this war orphan, his stateside assignment during the Vietnam War was as a casualty officer who notified the next of kin of a son or husband's death. Life had now placed him on the other side of the door.

I used to shave my head, and [they called me] the bald-headed major. The towns used to hate to see that Marine stock car come to town because it was another casualty call. I felt that maybe I was a little better prepared in having been through it myself. I guess in some way you can sort of second-guess what's going to come next, and it just got to be my routine. As much as you don't like doing it, it had to be done, and it really was our primary job for a while, especially 1969. I was stationed in Albany and I handled a bunch of reserve outfits. But my primary duty was casualty calls, and I would make the knock on the door.

I had the whole eastern part of New York State, eastern Canada, Vermont, and down as far as Westchester County. I didn't have New York City. Any killed in action, it was my responsibility to make that call. I could be called at three o'clock in the morning, and they would give me the details on the phone, and I'm on my way.

Then we had all the funerals, the firing detail, all that stuff, presenting the flag, and then there's the follow-up: insurance things and we had all the forms, too, the Social Security forms. So we would visit each family from the initial notification five or six times before it was finally wrapped up. The satisfaction came in knowing that it was done right.

My God! [How those small upstate towns suffered]. There was Amsterdam and Glens Falls. And a little town called Cherry Valley. They had three Marines and three killed. I buried two of them.

Even in retirement, death has continued to shadow John's life. One of his three sons committed suicide.

My third son, he did a hitch in the Marines, got out, and then not quite a year ago he committed suicide. He was having problems, and some of the kids he hung with over there were into drugs. He had problems in the service. I'm surprised they didn't throw him out. I have to say, I was very proud of him because he was working. I mean, he came out, he got a job as a carpenter's helper, and, of course, the building trade went sour. He was unemployed for a short period, and he got a job in a restaurant. . . . I saw him periodically. I talked to him periodically. I can look back and say maybe it wasn't enough, but what do you do? Then, I guess life just got too much for him.

His son's last action before his death was to lay out carefully on his bed his Marine Corps uniform, indicating that he wished to have a military service and to be buried in his uniform. For John Nichols, military burials have been the constant of his life.[3]

---

[1]For a summary of the 27th Division and the controversy that marked its role in the Saipan operation, see Ronald H. Spector, *Eagle Against the Sun: The American War with Japan* (New York: Free Press, 1985), pp. 312–17.

[2]For specific information on the circumstances of Major Nichols's death, see Edmund G. Love, *The 27th Infantry Division in World War II* (Washington, D.C.: Infantry Journal Press, 1949), pp. 328–32.

[3]Interview with Susan Hadler on August 31, 1993; AWON files.

John M. Nichols, 20 May 1944.

John M. Nichols with 27th Infantry Division in Hawaii, April 1943.

Nellie M. Nichols, 1946, in Ilion, New York.

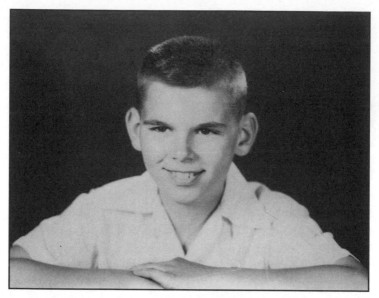

John E. Nichols, son of John M. Nichols. Age 12 in 1946, in Ilion, New York.

National Cemetery, "Punch Bowl," Hawaii.

Mary:

You're Out There on Your Own

ary's father, Edward C. Swaggerty, had already done a tour in the Army and was in the reserves when the Japanese bombed Pearl Harbor. The family was living in Tennessee, and he was listening to the radio when he heard of the attack. Mary recalls him calling to her mother:

"My God, Estelle, they bombed Pearl Harbor," and I thought—because we had just lived in Louisiana—Pearl Harbor was in Louisiana. So I was thinking, "Why would they want to bomb Louisiana?" Then it wasn't too long after that he was gone again. My Dad was thirty-three years old. He was one of the older ones. He was older than his lieutenant and everybody.

Edward Swaggerty served in the Army's 543rd Engineer Boat and Shore Regiment, which saw duty in New Guinea, the Bismarck Archipelago, and the Philippines. He died on 15 March 1945, near Zamboanga in western Mindanao, five days after the unit had arrived on the island. He had caught a ride on a barge going to another island. It struck a mine. Mary was seven years old.

141

At the time, the family received little information to explain what happened, leaving them with the impression that the government was hiding material:

My mother [thought] after my dad was killed—and I know I had the same impression—that the government probably lied to us, because there was no body, there was nothing except a telegram saying that he was missing and then three months later another telegram saying he was presumed dead. . . . So I just assumed that it was a big cover-up and that probably something different happened.

As a result, Mary would not be the only war orphan to wonder if perhaps her father were really alive:

We all felt like maybe he might be alive. My mother even dreamed that once, and I dreamed it a couple of times, that he was still over in the Philippines. Even my grandmother—she died in the fifties—said he was still alive, that he was not dead. He was coming back home.

There was such a void up there and such confusion, and maybe your mind just played tricks with you or whatever. He could have done this, he could have been here, he could have been lying out in the jungle and nobody knows that he's there. He could still be out in the jungle, thinking the war is still going on, all those things.

It would be many years later that Mary learned the details of her father's death. As an adult, Mary became determined to learn about her father. "All this information is out there, and I deam it's mine, and I want it." Inquiries into the government provided her only with a meager one-page military record of her father. An old family envelope, however, had "Company C" written on it. After multiple phone calls, she located the time and place of a reunion of her father's unit. And at the reunion she found one of the two men who had survived the barge's explosion.

My dad was just hitching a ride. He wasn't even supposed to be on the barge, [but] he had to go to another little island to do something. He just hitched a ride on this one. He was at the front of the ramp, rolling rope. He was squatting down, he and this other guy, when they hit the mine. It blew everything, and it blew them away from the wreck. My dad was closer to what they call the engine house, and all the rest of the guys were right there, and they were all killed. They thought they had cleared all the underwater mines out of the area. . . . When the mine hit the barge, it went everywhere, and there was a Navy boat not too far up, and they came down to assist right away. They got one body out, and that was the lieutenant's body, but the rest of them they couldn't find at all. There were six others that they could not find their bodies.

[The man] was telling me exactly where my Dad was standing when the impact happened and just the whole circumstances be-hind it and what led up to it and what their mission was when they were in this company. It made me understand—when you don't have any details about something, there's such confusion, and it was hor-rible. So I felt so good.

Mary brought her mother to the reunion, and together the two of them filled in pieces of Ed's wartime experience that neither had known:

Mom asked a lot of questions when she went to meet these guys, and they were so nice because they had all the memorabilia around in this room that they used at the time. They had all the maps of their objectives, from California all the way through New Guinea, the Philippines—all of their objectives all the way along. They explained every single one of them to us. It was wonderful, absolutely wonderful. It's just such a support system. Hey, my dad went here and he did this, he did that, and he did this. He wore a ball cap with the bill straight up in the Philippines when everybody else wore it down because it was so blessed hot you could hardly stand the sun. My mother asked all kinds of questions. She said it was very nice. She really enjoyed it.

To cap everything off, when I walked into the room with all these guys—and they were so nice to my mother and me—one guy came up and said to me, "I knew you were Ed's daughter the minute you walked through the door." That was the kicker. That was wonderful. That was the best thing ever.

It's almost like being with Dad because you're with the guy who was with him. See, that's what I wanted, and I told the guys when I went there, "One of the reasons I'm here is to put a personality to my dad which I never knew."

Mary's efforts to understand and heal did not stop at the reunion. She discovered that she could have a memorial marker for her father placed in Arlington National Cemetery:

I didn't know [about the markers] until I went with my mother-in-law just to tour the Cemetery. I asked the tour guide, "Those stones are really close together." He replied, "Yes, they're memorial markers for guys who were lost at sea." I said, "I had no idea you could have a marker erected here unless you had a body." And he said, "Oh, yes." I worked for the VA hospital in Hampton, Virginia, and I said "I'm getting on the phone, they owe me this." So they erected it, so I was really happy

My sister and I went a couple of months ago and took our breakfast and ate it out by the marker. So even though there's no body there, it's a representation of him. So we enjoyed it, we really did.

Like so much of Mary's life, however, the marker did not come easily or without a fight:

I'm so stubborn, I guess, that what I feel belongs to me, I'm not going to let anybody keep it from me. I don't care who I have to go over. [To get] the memorial I sent the paperwork off, and didn't hear and didn't hear. They said it would be about four weeks to two months, and at the end of that time, still nothing, nothing. And I kept calling, "Well, I don't know what the status is." Finally, I got the head guy who was in charge of these monuments, and he wanted to know how I got through to him. I said, "I don't know. I've just been very persistent because you people owe me this, and I want it." So he got on it, and it was erected within the month. They were just giving me the run-around. . . . so I just went to the top guy.

It had been a long journey for Mary and her family from March 1945 to that memorial marker at Arlington. Mary was the oldest of four children, with her only brother being the youngest. As a result, Mary has a few dim yet precious memories of her father. The other children have none:

My brother never saw my dad. My dad came home for his birth, and leave ran out and he had to go back to California, and then my brother was born three days later. So they never got to see each other. And my brother really missed him, because he grew up thinking that my dad preferred to stay in the Army rather than stay with us, because my mother never talked about it. Nobody ever talked about it. I just knew we were different because we didn't have a father and everybody else did.

I could remember a little bit about my dad. The only thing I can remember, I can visualize him, but I cannot remember his voice, and that bothers me so bad, because I cannot remember what he sounded like.

My aunt was just recently telling me that my uncle and he sounded exactly alike. Voice-wise, you couldn't tell them apart. So now I've got some idea of what his voice was like.

After he went back [into the Army], Dad only came home for one visit, and that was when my brother was supposed to be born. That's the last visual memory I have of him, of us being out in the yard and him fussing at me because I was messing with my cousin's new bike. He said, "You're going to turn it over, and you're going to scratch it," and I did. That's the only memory I really have of him, or the last memory.

The only other memory I can think of is when I was real little. He had a very protruding Adam's apple and an indentation underneath it, and he would lay on the floor, and I would crawl on top of him. I must have been around four or five, and I had some money, and I would put my money there and tell him that that was my bank. Those are the only two memories I have of him, and my sisters have none, and my brother has none. And that is so sad.

There was a void there always in my mind. To me, when I think of somebody, I get a mental picture. And when I would think of him, the picture would just get blurry. There is a person, but I just couldn't put a real definite face or voice or anything else. That was the thing that bothered me the most. No matter where I was, on March the 15th, every single year—and I wouldn't be thinking about it the day before or anything—it would pop into my mind that that was the day he was killed. No matter where I was. Every year. Today's the day, every year.

When Mary was a child, her father's brother made a comment that she neither forgave nor forgot:

[My uncle said] that he felt sorry for us, all of us kids, because we wouldn't amount to anything because my dad was gone. I was a very stubborn person to begin with, and I thought, "I'll show you, fella." And all of us did, because all of us went on to school after high school, and we all got some further education, so we did make something of ourselves. But I will remember that comment as long as I live. I must have been around eight or nine, somewhere along in there. He was quite concerned, so he said, about us making it. He didn't think we would because it was just my mother and all of us. That made me angry. But we did.

Mary's mother never remarried. Nor did she speak of her husband's death:

Mom never did talk about it, never. It's like he just never existed somehow, as far as conversation goes. I remember it was really hard for her and she was lonely trying to raise all of us. I remember her crying quite a bit. But I remember after that, she was like a general. I guess she just finally realized, "I've cried it out. Let's take care of this responsibility of all these children."

She said at one time that she kind of thought about remarrying, and she mentioned something to my sister. I was away from home by that time, but my sister said, "You do that, and I'll run away." My sister feels bad about making that comment now. Mom just had a lonely life.

Mary's mother concentrated her full attention on providing for her family:

Mom was a very strong woman, and she had four kids and one of my sisters has heart trouble and she was born with all these defects, and had to have open heart surgery when she was sixteen at Duke University and so forth. So my Mother had a real hard time raising all of us. She had to work and what-have-you.

The Veterans Administration representative in our little home town was not helpful at all. As a matter of fact, I went to school, but I had to do it with my aunt's help and my mother's help. We didn't know at that time that I could have gotten monies from the government. The representative did not tell us anything. He didn't tell my mother she could shop at Fort Bragg, and here she was trying to scrimp and save. It was just horrible. I just resent him so much.

Anyway, someone told Mom that she was entitled to some of these things, and then my second sister got to go to college with monies from the government, and my third sister did too. But I didn't, and it really made me angry. It's horrible. He was just one of the locals that I guess they sent him a few papers and said, "You're the VA rep for your area." And he didn't know beans, and it was just awful. My mother got a check from the government for money for us for living expenses, but as far as education or anything else, nothing. She didn't know we could go to the hospital at Fort Bragg, and my sister had to be taken to Duke every month. . . . So I just really resent the man. . . . But we made it, mainly because of my mother, who is such a strong person. I mean, she really was, to raise all of us and not get married, and keep her sanity. She's a sharp lady. . . . If she hadn't been strong, we would not have made it. We tease her today. We call her the Iron Lady.

The only male figure in the family was Mary's grandfather. The family had moved back to North Carolina and they lived with him for some years. Even when Mary's mother later learned that she was entitled to a VA loan for a house, and the family moved into a home of their own, Mary's grandfather lived right up the road. He provided the only father figure for the children:

He was a very old man. He was very kind and very gentle, and very good to us. My little brother called him "Poppa." As a matter of fact, when he was little and anybody would ask him who his dad was, he would say, "Winfield Scott Thomas," yet my brother's name was Swaggerty. They couldn't quite understand that, but he was our dad. So we did have an older, kinder gentleman around. But it still wasn't our dad. We really missed him. We really did.

Especially at night when I would go to bed, I thought about him almost every night. I just thought about how my life would have been different had he been here, and if my mother had been really on to me that day, she wouldn't have gotten by with this if my dad had been here. All the time. And if something went wrong at school, well, it wouldn't have happened had my dad been here. I used to even say that out loud at night, "If you had been here, this wouldn't have happened." You're out there on your own.

Though the family overcame many of the hurdles left by the death of her father, Mary believes that she and her siblings had been affected in ways that continue to the present:

We made it, like I said, but all of us in my family have had troubles in their marriages. My brother has had two divorces. I've had one. My sister and her husband haven't divorced, but they're just sort of "separate living," and then the other sister is a very religious sister, and they get along fine. But all the rest of us have had troubles. And I do believe it's because of Dad's death.

I married a Navy guy, and we traveled all over and raised our five kids and all that. Then, when that situation went by the way-side—and this is, again, my ex-husband's feeling—one of the reasons why we couldn't make it was because of my inability to know how to treat a husband. I don't know if this was an excuse or if it's for real. One of our psychologists that we went to talk to about our marriage said the same thing, that it probably was a factor, because I grew up in a house where there was no man. I had to learn an awful lot of how to deal with a marriage because I had no pattern.

Mary's quest for information about her father has been a vital, indeed necessary, part of her life:

I truly believe that you have to go through the mourning process—with marriages, divorces, deaths and what-have-you. And a real bad situation that happens to you—I still go through the stages to get rid of it and to file it away. . . . My two sisters felt the same way. My brother is still lost, I think. I took him up to see the marker at Arlington a couple of weeks ago, and he said it really meant a lot to him, it really did. But I still think he has not gone through the processes that I've gone through to file it away, and to get rid of it. It will always be there, but to file it, not to be so confusing.

My brother just doesn't really want to talk about it too much, and I can still sense the anger. He's got a lot of anger in him still, and I asked him, "Doesn't the way you feel"—he's very hyper—"don't you think that it has a lot to do with our dad?" He said, "Yes, I do, but I don't know what to do about it. And I don't know why it is," he said, "but it is." And I know it is, and it's caused him problems in his third marriage. I just would like for him to be at peace with himself about the whole situation because I believe that's his whole problem. I don't know what to do to help him. I've shared everything that I've gotten [about Dad] with him, . . . The only thing that he's done is gone to see the marker, and he said that did help him feel good about that.

I think his manhood is jeopardized somehow. I don't think he feels very manly, and I think he doesn't know how to hold on to relationships somehow. Maybe it scares him, I don't know. But I don't think he was ever taught sort of how to be a man either. My grandfather was too old. He was very docile and whatever. I just don't think he learned, and I think that's plagued him for his whole life.[1]

[1]Interview with Susan Hadler, November 6, 1993; AWON files.

(l–r) Back row, Mary Louise Swaggerty, Maggie E. Swaggerty. Front row, J. Carol Swaggerty, Thomas Edward Swaggerty, 1946.

(l–r) Maggie E. Swaggerty, Edward C. Swaggerty, and Mary Louise Swaggerty, 1942 in Louisiana.

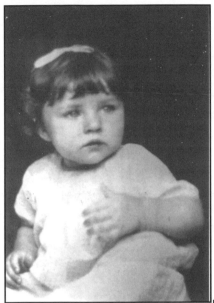

Mary Louise Swaggerty, 1937.

*Mary Louise Swaggerty Slowey at memorial marker
for her father, Arlington National Cemetery, 1992.*

★
★
★
★
★
★ **James:**
★ *The Lost Pilot*
★
_____
★
★
★
★
★ *J*ames Tate is a National Book Award and Pulitzer Prize winner for his poetry. His father, Samuel V. Appleby, flew with the 325th Bombardment Squadron, 92nd Bombardment Group, which was based in Podington, England. He died on a B-17 mission one month before the Normandy Invasion.

The Lost Pilot
for my father, 1922–1944

Your face did not rot
like the others—the co-pilot,
for example, I saw him

yesterday. His face is corn-
mush: his wife and daughter,
the poor ignorant people, stare

as if he will compose soon.
He was more wronged than Job.
But your face did not rot

like the others—it grew dark,
and hard like ebony;
the features progressed in their

distinction. If I could cajole
you to come back for an evening,
down from your compulsive

orbiting, I would touch you,
read your face as Dallas,
your hoodlum gunner, now,

with the blistered eyes, reads
his braille editions. I would
touch your face as a disinterested

scholar touches an original page.
However frightening, I would
discover you, and I would not

turn you in; I would not make
you face your wife, or Dallas,
or the co-pilot, Jim. You

could return to your crazy
orbiting, and I would not try
to fully understand what

it means to you. All I know
is this: when I see you,
as I have seen you at least

once every year of my life,
spin across the wilds of the sky
like a tiny, African god,

I feel dead. I feel as if I were
the residue of a stranger's life,
that I should pursue you.

My head cocked toward the sky,
I cannot get off the ground,
and, you, passing over again,

fast, perfect, and unwilling
to tell me that you are doing
well, or that it was a mistake

that placed you in that world,
and me in this; or that misfortune
placed these worlds in us.[1]

---

[1]James Tate, *The Lost Pilot* (New Haven, CT: Yale University Press, 1967), pp. 26-27.

Jim:

I Am the Father

---

*A*s the American forces pushed into Germany in late March 1945, the war in Europe had less than two months to its conclusion. Company B, 141st Infantry Regiment, 36th Division, was fighting just inside Germany, near the border town of Wissembourg, when one of its soldiers, Roy Warren Ehrler, was wounded and reported missing. His body was never recovered. He left behind a wife and a five-year-old son, Jim.

My dad was Missing in Action. It takes one year and a day for MIAs to be declared dead. The first thing I remember is my mom getting the government checks. That was how she was able to buy a house, with the insurance money. She worked in the shipyard. She was extremely shy, young, and vulnerable.

Conflict quickly developed between Jim's mother and grandmother over who would raise him:

Then there was a strange man [Jim's future stepfather] running through my house after my dad died. I remember to this day

155

my grandmother tried to take me away from my mother, and the police actually came down and arrested us and put us in jail. I was six or seven. My mom wasn't raising me right, according to my grandmother (my father's mother). I was the favorite son's son. My grandmother was going to raise me as his replacement. She had two sons. The other son hated her. He didn't forgive her until the day she died. She wasn't very popular. I didn't like her. I eventually abandoned that grandmother. She was a "no, no" to me.

We went to court, and the court asked me who I wanted to go with, my mother or my grandmother. Why in the hell would anybody in their right mind ask a seven-year-old who they wanted to live with? What if I had said my grandmother? What if I had said that? I would have gone home with her and lived with her. It makes me angry to this day. It was the damnedest thing I ever heard of. So my mother wasn't raising me right. It had nothing to do with my grandmother. Anyway, I told the court [that I wanted to stay with] my mother. My grandmother didn't particularly care if my mother was a good mother or not, she just wanted me. I am still upset about it fifty years later. Because I could have said, "I want to go to my grandmother's house, because we're going to do canning and stuff."

I don't think my mother was abusing me. I can't blame her for that. I don't think I am hiding anything or not remembering. She was sixteen years old. She came from a farm. They didn't socialize out there. She was fifteen when she was married. She didn't know anything. She didn't know how to raise herself, let alone a kid. But she was my mother. I loved both my mother and father.

Jim feels he raised both his mother and himself:

One of the things my mother said when my father died is "You are the man of the family." I took that seriously. And I was. My mother was not able to make good decisions. I became, at a very young age, *the* man of the house [emphasis in the original]. That was the beginning of the end for me and created problems for the rest of my life. My grandmother was basically right [about my mother's weaknesses as a parent]. Actually the war was the basic problem. If my father hadn't been killed in the war, I probably wouldn't have been trashed. But we don't know for sure what that would have been like. But I have no doubt I had something taken away from me. I didn't get to grow up like everyone else. Not only did I not have my father, I had to take care of my mother. I learned how to take care of me, too, which was way too young to learn to take care of me. So I became close to myself and I projected this strength to everybody. Everyone thinks I am very capable. And that's what I do.

My mother couldn't read. She couldn't learn to cook because she couldn't read a cookbook. I went to school and learned how to read, so I could read the cookbook. I learned how to cook. I started baking cakes from scratch by reading. My mother was awestruck that I could do that.

My mother was beautiful. I have photos of my mom and dad before he left. There is one of him and a buddy, too. But I am not sure I want to contact [the buddy]. It was fifty years ago, and I don't know what he would remember [about my dad]. If it was bad, I don't want to hear it. I have some questions in my mind about how I feel about actually trying to talk with him. I think if any of them had wanted to talk to me they could have found me. I haven't gone anywhere. None of them ever got in touch with my mom and said, "How are you doing? How's Jimmy doing?" Or anything. Everybody just wanted to get on with their life. Nobody cared about us. To hell with it. I think it was damn selfish. At least the government should have followed through on us.

We all went to school on the GI Bill, but it was like *Catcher in the Rye*. I was in one of the first classes to go to school on the Bill. They had just set that program up and they didn't want any failures, so they followed everybody really hard to make sure you got A's and stuff. Because we had to show this program really worked. My mother just happened to hear about the education program on the damn TV. And she called in, and that is how I got into it. You had to qualify for it. If she hadn't been listening to the TV, she never would have heard it.

It was the same when Vietnam came along. I didn't know that I qualified for an exemption from the draft as the only surviving son of someone who died in service. They let me sign up and still didn't tell me. They were going to draft me. I was on my way to Germany. I took some physicals but I had eczema so bad they let me back out. Then they sent me some information that they were going to test me again to see if I was better, and on those forms there was a little box to check if you were the only surviving son. And I checked it. But they were ready to send me.

Then I got a flash letter asking me what I meant by this? They said we don't have any records of your father ever being in the service. This was the same draft board who drafted me *and* my dad [emphasis in the original], and they had to have a record of it. I just came unglued and I got in touch with my mother. She came down to talk with them. It is not that I didn't want to serve, but I *did* my part [emphasis in the original]. I carry a lot of baggage because of it. If I had gone in and got killed, then that would have been the end of my dad's family line. . . . Anybody whose father was killed should not have to serve. That is the ultimate sacrifice: you lost your parent.

I went to school and became an architect, but I still have a hard time with that. I don't accept it that I am one, that I am good at anything. But I was mentored by a lot of different teachers who saw something in me. I was president of my senior class in high school. I had never had anyone telling me to do this or that, I just did it. It was an inner drive. I was going to succeed no matter what. But I made my own decisions to do it this way.

I talked to my dad when I was outside playing, and things like that. But I didn't share it with my mother or anything. My dad was a hero . . . like a god, because he wasn't there. He directed me. I was going to do what he wanted me to do, not what I figured out. Whatever I thought he wanted me to do is the direction I took. It gave me extra strength. It made me independent. I didn't give up. I drew extra strength from it. . . . The way I looked at it was I was here to take care of people. My mistake, probably. I did it to a fault. Now I am trying not to do that. That was how I "shared" with people. Now I try to do it differently.

My mother and stepfather didn't care what I did. They absolutely did not care. It didn't mean anything to them. I worked and made my own money by the time I was twelve years old. My mother got the [survivor's] money from the government every month, but it wasn't until my senior year that the government decided they wanted an accounting of where that money was going. Well, it was about time, because most of it was going for booze and some of it even went for child support for my stepfather's two daughters by another marriage. I knew it was happening and I resented that in my mother. It came between us.

My mother gave my dad's medals to my sister, even though my sister was not my father's daughter. So I had to buy some. It cost me $200 to buy the medals my dad had from dealers. A veteran gave me a list of the medals my dad should have had. So I was able to go to a store on First Avenue and just buy them because I knew what to get. When I was a kid I always wore my dad's medals around.

My stepfather was a drunk but he always showed up for work every day. My stepfather always worked. He made good money. My mom and stepfather had lots of money. I shouldn't have had to work. It was not necessary. First of all, the government was supporting me, and secondly they had plenty of money. Why was I working? Why did I give up my childhood to work while they sat at the local tavern? I never had a father. My stepfather was there, but he never participated in my life. As I said. I *am* the father [emphasis in original].[1]

---

[1]Interview with Susan Hadler and Ann Mix, August 1993; AWON files.

Roy Ehrler and unknown buddy on street in Rohrwiller, France, in February 1945. Written on back: "Me and another good Joe. Notice that German Pistol I've got."

Same street where Roy Ehrler and unknown buddy were photographed in Rohrwiller, France. Roy's son Jim Ehrler went to the village in 1995 and found a villager who helped him locate the street.

Roy Warren Ehrler in 1945, place unknown. Written on the back: "Ok, Valet, my trousers! Am a bit disappointed in the accomodations here. Not exactly Ritz-Carlton."

Roy Warren Ehrler as a civilian, hauling wood in Tacoma, Washington, in 1939.

James Leroy Ehrler (child) and Frieda Betschart Ehrler in 1941 in Tacoma, Washington.

James Leroy Ehrler, 1944 at Ocean Shores, Washington.

Roberta:
I Never Got to Know You

*J*ohn McCauley was a well-liked youth, blue-eyed, blond, and handsome, who played football in high school. "Jack," as he was called, had been orphaned as a young teen, and he and his twin brothers had been raised by relatives in Indiana. When he and his wife Lilly had a daughter, Roberta, in 1938, Jack was serving in the Navy and the family was living in California near the Long Beach Naval Station. Roberta was not yet four years old when the Navy declared John McCauley missing in action. She has only one shadowy memory of her father:

I can remember being an infant in a crib and seeing his outline against a lighted doorway. He seemed really huge. I can remember being in the crib, and I guess I was hollering because they had company and I didn't want to be left alone in the dark bedroom. So he came in and he gave me some gum. He kind of bribed me to be quiet. He gave me some gum, and I remember that. But that's about all. I really don't have a direct memory of knowing him.

McCauley served on the USS *Langley*. The ship had originally been built as a collier. In 1922, the Navy had converted her into the nation's first aircraft carrier. By the time of Pearl Harbor, however, the Navy had converted her again, this time into a sea plane tender, where she served with the Asiatic Fleet. On February 27, 1942, when the *Langley* was attempting to deliver fighter planes to Java, Japanese aircraft sank her. Escorting destroyers rescued the survivors, and only sixteen naval and aviation personnel were lost. The destroyers then transferred the survivors to the USS *Pecos*, a Navy oiler. But on March 1, Japanese aircraft struck the *Pecos* in three separate attacks, sinking her in mid-afternoon. This time the loss of life was very heavy. Whether Chief Petty Officer McCauley died during the original attack on the *Langley* or in the later attack on the *Pecos* is not known. The Navy simply notified the family that he was missing in action. In 1945, the Navy declared him dead.[1]

My mother told me she had a dream about this, and she dreamed that he was in the ocean or on a raft or something, and he was calling out to her. She dreamed that. She also had pictures of us taken. She and I both had on a black velvet dress with big white, lace collars, matching, and she had those pictures taken as a gift to him, and she sent them to him and they were returned. He never got them. . . .

My mother had a very rough time. . . . She really loved my father, and they had a good relationship, and he treated her well. She told me that she was a virgin when she married him, and she remained a virgin for four days. He coaxed her, but he was very respectful. There's a marvelous picture of the two of them that just looks like something from the *The Great Gatsby* or something, their wedding picture.

When the Navy declared Jack missing, his paychecks stopped. Since he was not yet declared dead, however, the family did not yet receive survivors benefits. This placed the family in financial limbo. Roberta and her mother lived in a modest house in California:

We had a little house there, and in later years I went back to see the house, and it seemed absolutely tiny, but at the time I thought it was okay. I remember living there with my mother. I remember that my mother was unhappy. She was a "Rosie the Riveter" and she worked. His paychecks were cut off after he was declared missing.

She told me later that she went to the Red Cross, and they might have given her a couple of little dresses for me or something like that, but they didn't really help. And I do remember going to nursery school. I remember standing at the blackboard in nursery school. I wasn't very tall, and we would draw airplanes, fighter planes with bullets coming out of them.

I can remember things like rationing coupons and these little round rationing things that they had and Victory Gardens and seeing newsreels about the war. So in 1980, when I visited Berlin, we were walking around the wall and we unexpectedly came to the Reichstag, and I somehow came across the Reichstag from the front, and I absolutely burst into tears because what flashed in my mind was I had seen this building in a newsreel as a child, with Hitler standing there and all those crowds screaming "Heil, Hitler," with arms raised in the Nazi salute, and there would be, like, millions of people. And I cried for hours. I couldn't stop crying, and was so surprised. I was so surprised at this reaction, so this was obviously something that was very repressed.

So you can't remember how you felt, or how upset you really were as a little child. I think then, too, that the adults were [thinking,] "You're a little kid and you don't understand what's going on." So they don't try to draw you out, they don't try to explain anything to you. You're just left alone. You're just left to your devices, and you're trying to figure out what's going on, but you just can't tell. . . .

I think there's one other thing I would say about those feelings of the infant and very young child and that is, after a lot of therapy, I could get in touch with almost everything, but there was still something I couldn't reach and that was the sense of guilt. The magical thinking of a three-year-old when a parent dies is that you killed that parent. You somehow murdered or killed that parent, and that you are in this magical thinking then, a guilty one, a murderer or a killer, and that you carry that, and it's so repressed. It's just down in your toes somewhere I think. I've not been able to access it and bring it up, because if I could do that, I think I could deal with it. . . .

When I was five, my mother found out that her mother had cancer. She lived on the East Coast. So Mother sold the little house in California. We had a little pink Chevy coupe, and I remember I had a little wicker chair, and I sat in the back, and she drove all the way from the West Coast to the East Coast. I was five years old. She left the West Coast because her mother was dying, and she didn't think my father was going to come back, but there was no official word.

We moved into my grandfather's house. It was a great big house, and my grandmother was quite ill in an upstairs bedroom. She died when I was six. She was laid out in the living room and a wreath was put on the door. People came to visit and to pay respects in the living room. So I was the only child in a household with four adults—my mother, her sister, and her father, and her mother who had just died. So it was kind of a lonely time.

By third grade, my mother remarried. I was almost nine. My stepfather had a German last name. I remember that it caused some difficulty when they were getting ready to be married, because I did not want to be adopted and I did not want to have a German last name because of all of this war propaganda to which I had been subjected. Germans and Japs, as they were called, were the enemy, and I felt very righteous about this. I mean, these were enemies.

Well, I knew that my father had died in the war, and the Germans and the Japanese were all of a piece. I was just as mad at the Germans as I was at the Japanese. I think that experience of saying "No, no! You're not going to be my father, you might be my mother's husband, but you will not be my father, I will not have your name," was really profound. They could not talk me out of that. Oh, they tried. My mother tried. I think she felt it would cause a problem and, you know, it's really a shame because it did cause a problem. However, I don't think it needed to. I think if the adults had been bigger and more spacious, they could have understood how I might have felt. But as it was, they didn't see that, so it did cause a problem.

In the beginning of the marriage things were delicate. I guess I felt the tension. I may have felt resentful at levels that I wasn't completely aware of. Later, when my mother and stepfather were having many, many marital problems, she would refer back to that time. When she was thinking of marrying him, people had warned her that he would not treat me well and that there would be difficulty and problems. I don't know whether they said that because the sense they had from him or because they just felt generally stepfathers and stepkids just don't get along. I don't know. There were warnings.

With her mother's remarriage, Roberta found her position changed. The family moved to the Midwest, and the three family members soon became four:

When I lived in the East, I was big cheese. Being in a household with four adults who kind of watched over you and every move you made and everything you said and everything you did, I was the focus of a lot of attention. . . . In that household, I really was special. . . . I was number one child, and I had a certain status. Even though my mother later had other children, they never, ever measured up to my status in those people's eyes. . . . Then when mother remarried, I was supposed to accept it, and I didn't like this at all. So I went from being the center of this household to being the stepchild.

We moved in with my stepfather's parents. My mother was pregnant with my sister, who is nine years younger than I am. My mother and stepfather had four children about two years apart, three daughters and a son. Later, when I was going through therapy, I learned that I had become a parental child, because my mother was the youngest of three children and when this happened with my father, she was the baby, and somehow I ended up taking care of her, rather than the other way around. I don't know quite how that happened, but it did.

My stepfather's parents did not like my mother and they did not like the idea that he married a widow with a child. He was their number one son, and he wasn't supposed to do that. That was not a fitting match for him by their lights, and they were upset. They did not treat her well. Then when my sister was born, the attention focused on her.

The family then moved to the country and raised chickens and other animals for food:

We lived with his parents for about a year or so. Then we bought an acre. There was a house, a one-bedroom house and a large, two-car garage, and a half-acre planted in hay. We moved out there. My mother and stepfather slept in the living room, and my sister and I were in the bedroom. . . .

We had animals. We had rabbits and chickens and, unfortunately, they kept these animals because they didn't have much money. My stepfather was working as an electrician. He would kill these rabbits, and he would force me to be there while he cut off the heads of the chickens and plunged them in boiling water and things. He forced me to hold the light when he did this after dark. The mother rabbit sometimes ate the baby rabbits up, and they had to be killed because they were half-eaten and they were still alive, so I would be given the job of drowning the baby rabbits in a bucket. I was made to carry buckets of chicken intestines to neighbors for their dogs.

Before the family had moved to the Midwest, Roberta had been infected with head lice at the Catholic school she had attended. Now, with the arrival of her new sister, her mother and stepfather treated her as if she were still infected:

I was told I was "contaminated." The way they played that out was that I couldn't touch food and I couldn't prepare food. My laundry was washed separately from the other people's laundry in the family. If I took a shower, my mother had to take a shower in between my stepfather taking a shower and my taking a shower. . . .

I was not allowed to touch my sister. Well, I would sneak. I remember one time scaring myself to death, because I picked her up and I didn't know how to do it. Her body went all the way back, and I thought, "Oh, my God, I've injured her."

I just wanted to hold her. I had terrible self-esteem. I just felt alone and nobody could relate to me. I got really strong about being alone, which is obviously a double-edged sword. It has a lot of positive aspects. I can stand up and do things where other people would just fold. But, on the other hand, it's been a real loss in life. . . .

I was treated as an untouchable, and it was played out. My stepfather was not physically abusive. I think there was some time when he beat me for something or other, but I wouldn't give him the satisfaction of making a sound. So that was not rewarding, so he didn't do that. But I guess the emotional abuse must have been more rewarding.

I was just upset all the time. I would try to avoid him. I did not like him. I tried to stay away from him.

The family sold the house and bought some land further out in the country. Roberta's stepfather began to build a house. It took him thirty years to complete it:

He built the whole thing himself, every nail, everything. But at the time, they sold the property where we were living, and they moved into a garage across the street. It was just like a two-room garage sort of thing, a garage that had been converted into an apartment. It was at that point—I was about twelve by then—I remember begging my mother I wanted to leave. I couldn't stand living there.

My relatives back East had said that I could come and live with them, and eventually she said that I could go. And do you know, I never forgave her for letting me go. . . . I was basically away for the seventh and eighth grade. By the ninth grade, I was back at home, and I stayed there until I graduated from high school. . . .

When I was sixteen, I had a bed that was in a store room. Over the bed was a clothes line where they hung my clothes. Next to the bed was the tank that held the propane or oil or whatever that they used for heating, the fuel that was used for heating was in my bedroom. And then there were shelves around that were full of boxes of material—my mother sewed—canned goods and storage. It was the storage room, and this was all underground because he was still building the house. And there were two other bedrooms. They had one bedroom, the two of them, and then the other four children had the other bedroom. There were two sets of bunk beds. I had slept in there for a while, but when the last child came, then I had to move into the store room.

It was not good that mother had more children. He was being very abusive to her. He was hitting her, and then she would complain to me and, naturally, I just thought he was a monster. I mean, I had no perspective at all. He was a monster, she was wonderful and the poor victim, and I continued to feel all this compassion for her. She was the victim. I had really good training on how to be a victim, masterful training. "What can I do?" she would say. "I can't leave him. I have no means of support. I have all these children." She was Catholic. She wouldn't use birth control and kept having all these children. So she painted it as a completely hopeless situation. She could do nothing, and I really suffered for her.

Roberta's greatest outlet was at school where she was an "A" student and member of the National Honor Society. With the help of a scholarship and money from her father's insurance policy, she continued her education beyond high school, ultimately earning a Ph.D. Relations with her mother, however, became more strained. After Roberta had married and had her second child, her mother asked her to do something that Roberta felt should not be done. Roberta refused:

She went through the ceiling. She said, "You don't love me, you don't care about it," and all this stuff. And do you know, we didn't speak for a year and a half.

During the time I was getting my Ph.D., she went to a priest and tried to have me excommunicated from the church for not bringing up my children Catholic. . . . Can you imagine? I was thirty-eight years old at the time. The priest told her to forget it.

Earlier my mother had talked about my stepfather being afraid that my father was going to show up after they were married, some day, somehow he emerges from the jungles on one of the South Sea islands and comes back to claim her. So that was the fear for several years. Then gradually what happened is that he became very interested in the history of the war. He had been at Pearl Harbor and survived Pearl Harbor, and has stories to tell about that. And he's kind of become an ally of my mom's. When I mentioned this thing about a war orphans' network to my mother, she responded, "Well, I want to know about that. Keep me informed about that," and so on and so forth, and I thought, "No way. This one is mine."

Several years ago when Roberta discovered that the government would supply a marker to the family of anyone who was missing in action, lost at sea, or whose body was not recovered, she applied for the marker and a held a ceremony for the immediate family:

I went and actually arranged a plot for my father in the local cemetery. I arranged to have the marker set into the ground and I had a tree planted there and arranged a ceremony and a small reception at my house. I called the university ROTC and arranged for a Navy bugler to come over, and my husband's father, a minister, came, and I think my mother wrote something to be read at this. We put together our own ceremony. This was a private thing.

It was a small group, and it rained. Wouldn't you know? So here we are with the umbrellas and we had this service for him and things were read.

And my mother came unhinged. She just absolutely cried like this had just happened. She wailed. She howled. It was like things you would see in Europe or you know, where the women cut loose and they just scream and wail at the top of their lungs. That's what she did, like an animal. It was the only ritual that there ever was that she attended that marked his passing.

I was so taken aback by what she did. I was glad that we did it, but I don't think I completely got through that myself. I'm a great believer in the importance and value of rituals to mark passing of stages in life and seasons in life. I think that was one of the best things, developmentally and in the healing process, that could have been done. So long overdue.

I think everyone was taken aback by how stricken she was. She had to be assisted back to the car. And I think she really had to gather herself back together in order to go back to her life, because she had to go back to the current husband. And if you understood how she had come unhinged, she really loved my father.

Nor was the marker the only healing move Roberta took:

When my stepfather and my mother were in their early to mid-70s, I thought it would be a good idea to put together a memory book, which meant a page from every member of the family, as a gift. The page could be anything. It could be photos or a letter or a collage, pictures, drawings, poems, anything. I sent pages all over the country, and then each grandchild and each child got one in the mail and sent them back in time for Christmas. Then my sister and I assembled them right before Christmas, and we wrapped them up. I had an artist friend do the calligraphy on a contents page and everything. It was very nice.

On Christmas Day, I had flown in from wherever I was. We were sitting in my brother's living room, and they were sitting on the couch, and they opened up these gifts, side by side, and they began to look at them and realize what they were. And they both started crying. They both broke down in tears. And we had to get the Kleenex. They were just sobbing. They were very difficult people. To get this expression of love instead of hostility was kind of overwhelming.

My step-father reached out to me and said—totally in tears and barely able to speak and putting his arm out—"I feel so bad about the way I treated you when you were a little girl. I didn't know and I didn't realize, and if I had it to do over, I would do it differently. Please forgive me."

I was just thunderstruck. I had no concept or intimation that anything like this would occur. I replied, "Of course, I forgive you," which was completely spontaneous. How could you not forgive someone who asks?

So again, it was a healing thing, and—because members of the family witnessed this—I really think it changed the dynamics. And my mother had also asked forgiveness in a different way at an earlier time in a letter. I think a lot of healing has gone on.

Roberta worked in therapy to resolve her feelings about her parents. As part of the therapy, there was an exercise with an empty chair where Roberta expressed her feelings to her father as if he were actually sitting in the empty chair:

My overwhelming feeling was fury and anger. I really wanted to let him have it, and I just shouted and yelled at him. I told him how furious I was with him for going off and getting killed when I was little and leaving me to care for my mother. That was *his* job [emphasis in original]. I screamed, "This was your job, and I got stuck with this." I went on about this at length, and articulated a lot of anger.

"And I never got to know you. I never got to know the positive side of you. I heard you were such a neat person." I had spent time with friends of his who gave me a little airplane that he made out of shell casings and stuff. It's an artifact. They gave it to me, and their faces just shone when they described him and their relationship with him. So I was mad that I didn't get to know him, and I was telling him this. And I had the sense that he was sort of watching this from on high, listening, and he was sort of witnessing all this anger. And he was not upset. . . . And I felt a lot better. He seemingly had acknowledged my feelings, and I tried very hard to let him go. I felt that I had been trying very hard to hold on to him for a very long time, and my job was to let go, to try to go through this and try to let go of him.

Later, Roberta's church held a Holy Eucharist for her father, a religious ceremony that she felt held special meaning to her:

This was the ritual that was, I think, more meaningful to me than the marker service that was more meaningful to my mother. I remember being up in front and the rector saying that this mass was dedicated to my father. And there were a lot of parishioners there, and we went through it.

I don't think I'm totally free of the past, but I'm much freer than I was. I don't think this is something that one will completely recover from—all one can do is hold it differently. That's what I've come to conclude. You hold it differently.[2]

[1]For further information on the *Langley* and *Pecos*, see Volume III, *The Rising Sun in the Pacific, 1931–April 1942* (Boston: Little, Brown, 1948), pp. 359–363 and 378, of Samuel Eliot Morison's *History of United States Naval Operations in World War II*. It is perhaps symptomatic of the lack of information that many orphans have of the circumstances and details of their fathers' deaths that Roberta, in her interview with Susan Hadler, thought that the *Langley* sank north of Guam.

[2]Interview with Susan Hadler, May 5, 1994; AWON files. Roberta is not her real name, as she requested anonymity.

Jeff:
I Expect People to Die on Me All the Time

$\mathcal{J}$eff's father, Harold Luckey Ward, Jr., served as a waist gunner on a four-engine B-17 bomber. Almost everyone called Harold "Luckey." He grew up in Pelham, New York, and had attended Syracuse University for two years. Harold then worked as a purchasing agent in New York City. He met Jane Hooper, and they married in January 1941. Eight months later he enlisted in the Army Air Force. With his enlistment, his new bride moved in with her parents in their home at Garden City, New York, while Harold completed his training. Jeff was born in Garden City in February 1942.

Jane and Jeff followed Harold through some of his training in Florida and California. When he went overseas, Jane went back to her parents and stayed in their large house in a middle-class area built in the 1930s. Jeff's earliest memories date to this house and a family which included Jeff, his mother, his grandmother and grandfather.

Luckey Ward, a member of the 331st Bombardment Squadron, 94th Bombardment Group, died on October 20, 1943. It was his second combat mission. Not until 1994, when Jeff received two letters from one of his father's crew, did Jeff learn the circumstances of the death:

175

Your Dad, Luck[e]y Ward, was one of the best friends I ever had. We always went together wherever we went. In fact, our crew was a "tite-nit" crew. We were always together whenever possible. If one went to town, we all went. It is hard for me to describe your Dad after so many years.

I first met your Dad in Blythe, California. It is on the edge of Death Valley. They told us we were lucky to be there in the rainy season but I never saw so much as a drop of dew all the time we were there. We lived in tents with canvas cots for beds and believe it or not, we were issued wool blankets. It remained about 120° day and night. There was always just enough air moving to keep the sand stirred up. You would go to sleep and wake up when the sand slid off your face into your eyes.

They assigned us to crews at that time. I was Flight Engineer and top turret gunner. Sgt. Ward was left waist gunner. . . . Luck[e]y and I went with a substitute crew on the October 14th Schweinfurt raid, which was a real test of courage.[1] We had eight hours of constant enemy fighter attacks. Luckey held up real well and proved himself worthy. The second raid, we went as a complete crew to Duran, Germany [Düren is east of Aachen]. That wasn't so good. We dropped our bombs, then sustained a burst of flack that knocked out our No. 2 engine, our radio and our oxygen system. We still had some oxygen but at 29,000 feet we were using it fast. My own system in the turret was gone completely. The co-pilot gave me his portable bottle that I hung on my belt. The pilot ordered me to transfer the fuel out of our leaking No. 2 engine. I was down on my knees at the bulkhead when we sustained a rocket hit from an enemy fighter. The controls were jammed and we were on our way down. The pilot gave the "bail-out alarm" and we put on our parachutes. The cockpit crew were to go out through the open bomb-bay doors. This is where my conscience bothers me a little. I was to be the first one out of the bomb doors, but I tried to figure a way to get through the bomb racks without removing my parachute so I could see how the rest of the crew were doing [the only way to pass through the bomb-bay area on a B-17 was to walk along a narrow catwalk; the catwalk did not allow enough room for a crew member to wear his parachute]. As I hesitated in the door, the co-pilot came through without his oxygen, being that I had his. He thought I was afraid to jump so he put his hands on my shoulders and pushed me out. As far as I know everyone in the plane was all right when I left it, but according to reports, the co-pilot and I were all that made it. I tried to pull my rip cord as soon as I could so I could watch the plane but that was a mistake. The oxygen bottle hit the end of the hose so hard it pulled the hose clear out of the mask. Either the snap of the band around my neck or the lack of oxygen caused me to pass out and I never saw or heard the plane nor the rest of the crew.

I have always felt maybe I could have tried harder to get to them [in the waist and rear of the aircraft]. The report was that the plane blew up after two parachutes were seen. I suppose the co-pilot saved my life but I swear to you that the others were all right or I would never have left the plane without them. Never for a moment should you doubt the integrity and courage of your Dad.

Your Dad was very loving of you and your Mother and that was his continual thought. Get the war over so he could come back to the two of you. He was very faithful to you and your Mother and never stepped across the line. I know, because I was with him every time we went on pass.

I came home from prison camp very depressed, but soon found a very good wife that helped me immensely. . . . I broke my neck and back when I parachuted so I was very fortunate to have survived and to be able to work at all . . .

Sincerely,
Clifford Horn

For Jeff and his mother life went on. The impact of Luckey's death and his absence within the family permeated their lives, however, as it would permeate so many lives of orphans and widows of the war.

I lived with my mother and my grandparents because my dad never came back. When he left for overseas he told his cousin that he wasn't coming back. He knew that he wasn't going to make it. After the war was over my uncle and grandfather went over to Europe and identified the body. So they had come up with a body. He had broken his shoulder when he was younger and that is how they identified him. The Germans kept very good records. He is buried in Belgium, and I haven't been to see his grave.

My mother and I lived in an area where we knew everybody. We even knew the postman. So the postman got the death notice and knew what it was. He waited several days until he felt it was the right time to deliver it.

My mother never got over my father's death because they were married young. She loved my father and thought he was the most wonderful person in the world. She kept putting him on a pedestal. She did do some dating but that was never successful. She dated a Canadian officer. My great aunt had a farm in Nova Scotia, and we would go up and visit them. That is how mother got involved with this man. But she always told me she didn't marry him because of me. I was very difficult. I cried a lot and was a real pain in the ass. I remember one time—we were there a couple of summers—being very upset about wanting to do something and not getting to do it and making such a scene. I had a lot of problems, just problems.

So I just grew up in a world without a father. I had no knowledge of or identification with my father. But we always ran into the inevitable father-and-son baseball game and such. My mother always made sure somebody would be in the area, somebody who could take me out or be a "father." Some of them were family, some were people that she knew in the area. That was always an issue, that I didn't have a father. I remember that became an issue. I don't remember bringing it up, but it was always sort of there.

Jeff never knew much about his father or his father's family. His paternal grandfather died when he was four years old.

Harold, Sr., committed suicide in 1946. He went into the garage, closed the door and turned the car engine on. I don't know why he killed himself. It could have been because of my father or because he didn't do well in business. I didn't even know he killed himself until about ten years ago. My father's side of the family was kind of strange. My mother's family didn't like my grandfather. I knew that growing up.

I grew up with adults. My family never talked about anything. You don't talk about religion, about politics and you certainly don't talk about family—particularly family. They were middle-class tight-lipped Yankees! I called my grandparents Granny and Grandpa but I always called my mother by her first name, Jane.

Mother and I lived on Long Island with her parents until I was about ten. Then they retired and sold their house, and we moved to the middle of Garden City into an old apartment house, a big walk-up. It was a big building, a block long. We lived on the fourth floor and we used to go up on the roof a lot at night and sit and look at the lights.

My mother was drinking heavily after the war, I guess, and heavily in the early fifties. She was an alcoholic, and when we moved out of the house where I grew up her drinking got worse. She was a big woman, five feet nine and 140 pounds. Big boned. But she was sick a lot. She had her thyroid out and a hysterectomy when she was thirty-four years old. She was having a lot of pain. I figure she had cirrhosis of the liver by then because her pain was in the back and in the liver area. She had migraines constantly. She ate and ate aspirin.

She never participated in any of the veterans or memorial days parades. She was entitled to sit in the reviewing stand but she wouldn't do it. She was very bitter toward the government because she felt it was their fault.

When we moved, then she started really drinking. She would send me out to buy beer, forgetting I was a minor. I was hiding bottles [from her] for a long time. I used to put them out on the porch. When she would have a problem I would call my uncle up, and then they would come down and take care of her. Once me and the neighborhood kids found her drunk in the parking lot next to one of my neighbors. She was so puffy and bloated the kids in the neighborhood didn't even recognize her. I got all the kids out of the way and called my grandparents. They came over and cleaned her up. My grandfather used to blame her drinking on me. He used to call me a coward.

Then on June 18, 1954, we had stayed up late the night before and we talked. She had been upset about some things, and I was very frank with her and said something that upset her. We planned [that] I was going to skip school, and she and I were going to go to Jones Beach the next day. So I sacked in. About 7:30 in the morning I woke up and there was the superintendent standing in the doorway. He was Catholic and he had his priest with him. I said to myself, "Oh shit." I knew something was wrong and that it was my mother.

He had found my mother. She had jumped off the back of the building onto the pavement in the parking lot. They just told me my mother had died and the priest was there to help me. They took me out the back of the building, but I guess they had already taken her away. I went to a friend's house for a few days and they were very comforting. My classmates came by and gave me a baseball glove and told me they missed me. Not being one of the more popular kids in class, that was very nice. Then a couple days later, after the funeral, I was temporarily taken to Norfolk, Virginia, where I was to stay with my mother's brother. Later, they helped raise me.

Mother left a rambling note in green ink, using a ruler. It said she was in pain. She was sorry. But that was about it. I don't remember it. A few years ago I destroyed that note, which was probably a mistake. Recently I wrote to the police and the only record they had was the police blotter. It read, "7:25 am Phone Call from Veronica H . . .wife of the superintendent of Franklin Apartments reported a woman lying on the sidewalk in the rear of the apartment apparently dead . . . Dr Fulltz notified. Pronounced Jane Ward, age thirty-four, apt 3–L 223 7th Street, dead."

The funeral was at a funeral home not too far from where my mother and I lived. The chapel was on the second floor. I remember going in the rear of the building and there were steps that went up to the second floor. There was a closed casket. I never saw my mother, which was a mistake. I had a Bible, the New Standard Revised edition, and I sat on the right side in the first seat in the front aisle. I remember hearing people behind me saying it looks like he is going to weep. I could barely stand. There was a short service. I asked that they read second Corinthians, verse 13. The one about love.

Then we all went downstairs and got in the funeral-home cars and drove into the city. We went to a big building. The floors were concrete. You walked in the rear, and it was shaped like a cross. You could go right, forward, or left. We went to the left, and there was a viewing room. They had a carpet we stood on and there was a screen that opened. We stood there and my mother's casket went by on rollers and into the fire, into the furnace, where we watched it burn. My mother's brother, who was in the Navy, was given the remains and at some point in time, when he was at sea, he held a small ceremony and threw, deposited, sprinkled them. He did that, and it seemed like the right thing to do.

After my mother died, my grandfather made it very clear that it was my fault she committed suicide. "It's your fault," he said. I was twelve. Your brain knows it's not true, but I always kinda felt if I had stayed awake, or if we hadn't talked, or hadn't done all this stuff that night before, that she wouldn't have done it. Today I know if I had stopped it that day it would have been the next day. But it was hard to kinda put all of this together. Every year they recognized her death date. They celebrated her death, if you will, her death date. And if I didn't—when I was older—send remembrance flowers, or remember to call, it was the great family tragedy for the year.

As an adult, Jeff's expected annual contact with his grandparents on the day of his mother's death would continue until they died. Following his mother's suicide, Jeff lived first with his grandparents, with his grandfather becoming his guardian, and later with his uncle.

There was money for me from my father's estate but my grandfather was just taking the money and didn't buy me clothes or anything. We were always just scraping by. But I didn't care. After a couple of years my grandparents got into a huge fight and moved down to Virginia Beach. So I went to live with my uncle in Norfolk. When I lived with my aunt and uncle they wanted to adopt me. I didn't have a problem with that except I didn't want to change my name. So I said, "Well, no, because I don't want to change my name."

Jeff spent his remaining dependent years living with his aunt and uncle. He kept his father's name. He later graduated from college and law school, and now is married and has two sons. Although he struggled to put the tragedy of his mother and father behind him, trying hard to accept it and move on with his life, Jeff eventually sought counseling.

I just really hadn't done much with my father. That had always just been kind of there. I was very self-conscious about that. I never talked about my mother. I just didn't. I would say she died of cancer or something else. It wasn't until the 1970s I started talking about her just to a few people. I never could really get mad at her for doing that. It just kind of dissipated instead of coming out. But I know for years I would think about her every day. I guess you feel guilty because you haven't done anything to make it better. But you don't really know what to do. So you are just stuck there. I am not real fast about things. I've always had trouble dealing with it. I would like to but I have trouble. When my mother died I never saw her body. It is very important when people die to see the body. You see something. You have to see something.

I didn't know what closure was. After some years in therapy I learned the wisdom of it. I guess there never was closure. It takes a while, and you can't do it systematically as the textbooks say. If someone dies today, you go through all those steps and you can document them. I had put everything aside about my father. Then in my thirties I started working on it. When you don't tackle it for twenty years and then work on it you don't go through those four stages as clearly defined as they may be in a book. When you start tackling this twenty or twenty-five years later you are in denial. But you don't stop denying and go to the next step as clearly as you may do if someone dies today. It's much more ragged. It's not organized. That's bothered me, because I never could get a handle on it. I can't say, "Okay, I finished denial. Now I go to the next stage." And it never happened. And with a father, never having seen him, you can't deny—and then the other part of it is you get mad at someone for leaving you. And I've always had difficulty with that.

I remember fantasizing for years that my father lived in South America. I'd run into him in a bookstore in Venezuela. He was working for the CIA. I knew that was silly. I knew it was a game. When my mother died, I never saw her. I never saw the body. You see something, you have something. I had aunts die and the closed coffin, and I wasn't sure if they had died. I said, "You have to open the coffin. I have to see the body."

One thing I always did. I got it from my family and I even do it to this day. Whenever anybody mentions they were born in the 1920s, I always count to see if they were in the war. I always do that. I find "war orphan" to be an interesting term because it's really not fair to the woman, because it's as if both parents were killed in the war. But I guess both my parents were. My father was twenty-eight and my mother was thirty-four when they died. I expect people to die on me all the time. I used to kill people off in my mind so I could cope with them when they did die, and I used to expect to die young myself.[2]

[1]Schweinfurt, in southeast Germany, held much of the German ball-bearing industry. At the time, this target lay beyond the range of American fighter planes, so bombers had to fly without fighter escort for much of the attack. On the raid of October 14, 1943, German defenses shot down 60 of the 229 bombers that attacked the target, placing American losses at over 26 percent. A further 17 bombers had to be scrapped after limping back to their English bases. For a further discussion of Schweinfurt, see Stephen L. McFarland and Wesley Phillips Newton, *To Command the Sky: The Battle for Air Superiority over Germany, 1942-1944* (Washington, D.C.: Smithsonian, 1991), pp. 127-133.
[2]Interviews with Susan Hadler, October 1993, and with Ann Mix, September 1995; letters of Clifford Horn, April 20 and August 30, 1994; AWON files.

Jeffrey Luckey Ward and his father, Harold Luckey Ward, Jr., in their backyard in Garden City, New York, 29 July 1943.

Sargeant Harold Ward (top row, third from right) in 1943, along with several of his buddies, in front of Ward's B-17, "Sharpe's Wagon."

The Ward family in their backyard in Garden City, New York, 29 July 1943. Harold Luckey Ward, Jr., Jeffrey Luckey Ward, and Jane Hooper Ward.

Sargeant Harold Ward inside a B-17 at Army Air Force Base in Dyersburg, Tennessee, May or June 1943.

Sheila:

My Father Probably Never Knew That I Had Been Born

For Sheila, World War II meant not only losing a father, but a mother as well. She was an orphan in the more commonly understood sense of the term. She recalled her childhood in a letter and phone interview to the AWON:

I was adopted out of the Catholic Children's Foundling Home in New York. I had been taken there by my mother when I was one-year old. My mother was one of twelve children whose Catholic family immigrated, when she was a child, from Ireland to New York City. She was cast out of her Catholic family by her irate mother when she became pregnant by a young Navy seaman on his way to the war in the Atlantic. My father died when his ship was torpedoed by a German U-Boat. My young unmarried mother was left on her own to raise me. I believe my father probably never knew that I had been born.

Her adoptive parents later told her of her natural mother and the conditions that led to Sheila's arrival at the Foundling Home. She has tried to be understanding of her mother's plight and of the circumstances that led to her mother's actions:

My mother struggled to survive as a single parent unaided by her family. Eventually she met someone and fell in love again. She was asked to marry but the man did not want the responsibility of another man's child. My mother decided to give me up for adoption so that she could remarry. When I was one year old I was given to the Catholic Foundling Home in Manhattan.

I have no recall of my experience living in the Foundling Home or of the four foster homes in which I lived for short periods of time. Nor do I recall the abuse at one foster home that brought me to the hospital. A ten-year-old child put me on a hot radiator. My leg was badly burned, and the wound became infected from lack of attention. A case worker noticed me limping when she visited the home and, upon checking the condition of my leg, immediately took me for medical attention and out of my foster parents' custody.

I sometimes dream of being on a gurney in a hospital and being wheeled down a long hall with flashing ceiling lights overhead. I had this dream off and on throughout childhood and believe that it was the true experience of being brought to the hospital. My leg still shows the scars of this experience. Beyond this memory is nothing that I can recall prior to being adopted.

Good fortune came to Sheila when a childless couple adopted her as well as two boys whom the war had orphaned:

My adoptive mother worked as a foster mother for the Catholic Hospital and was there when I was brought in for my burns. My condition and circumstance touched her, and she volunteered to take me home. She and her husband, unable to have children of their own, applied to adopt me after one year. I have nothing but good things to say about my adoptive parents. They were older than parents would normally be and they were kind to me. What I remember most about going to live with them is feeling incredibly safe and secure.

My adoptive parents, within a short time, adopted a total of three children from the same home. Each child had a father who was killed in World War II. Besides myself there were two boys who were born within months of each other. Our adoptive parents more than made up for our unsettled beginnings. They were Catholics who attended church regularly and sent us to Catholic schools. Our adoptive mother stayed home and, although not physically demonstrative, showed caring in her constant dedication to our well being. Our adoptive father, who was a police officer, was loving, warm and outgoing. He was easy to talk to about anything. Both our adoptive parents were stable and consistent and taught us values of the old fashioned kind.

Because of my adoptive parents, I feel today that, despite my bad beginning, I have turned out with a minimal amount of psychological damage. I do admit that there is some damage, however, like being wary of strangers and having a certain "detachment" to my personality. I do not trust easily and and I do not like to reveal too much about myself. I feel that these things are a result of being put in foster homes and the abuse I experienced there.

Sheila would sometimes carry these characteristics into her adult relationships:

When I met my husband for the first time I went slow and checked him out to see how stable he was and how much of a secure life he could provide. We dated through letters for over a year, and I felt that I knew him well before marrying him. Although he was a military man and we have traveled around the world, I have felt safe and secure wherever I went with my husband and found our travels interesting.

In looking back at her life, Sheila believes that events ultimately worked out for the best:

I have three children and feel that I was given the skills to be a good parent. The children are doing well. Overall, I feel lucky to have been adopted and am happy with the way things turned out. In fact my life story is pretty boring. I think that if I had stayed with my birth mother my life would have been much harder and feel that my birth mother did the right thing for me by giving me up. I have no desire to look for her.

Sheila, however, has long desired to know more about her father, that unknown sailor on an unknown ship.

I have had, over the years, a fascination with my father. But I promised myself that I would not pursue learning anything about him until both my adoptive parents were dead. After they died, I began to search for information about my father. His name was on papers that I had from the hospital, and I was told by my adoptive parents that he was killed in the war.

I tracked down a great deal of information on one war casualty with the same surname, including the acquisition of a photo of him, and it was clear he couldn't be my father. I have since tracked down information about the only other man killed with my father's surname and am now satisfied that he is the right man. He was twenty when he went down in his ship at sea in the fall of 1943 with fifty-one others from the ship's crew.[1]

Although she understands why her mother gave her up for adoption and hopes that she had a good life, Sheila still has an ambivalence about her mother's action, and that ambivalence perhaps holds a key to why she wants to know about her father:

I don't exactly know why I want to know about my father and not my mother, except that I feel a deep hurt because my mother gave me up as a child so that she could marry a man who made it clear that he did not want to take care of another man's child. And, interestingly enough, my adoptive father was willing to accept not one war orphan, but *three*! [emphasis in the original]

    Sheila later wrote to Ann Mix on the subject of being an adoptive child and whether or not to search for one's birth-parents:

I can understand in a way an adoptee's "need," if you will, looking into their background. But I honestly feel that in many ways, it can be very damaging to a relationship between a child and the adoptive parents to search while they are living. Also, many women who give up a child do it for various reasons, and I'd hate to be the one who finds a parent and is rejected. There are not that many happy endings. Also, if an adoptee meets a parent, and the parent is receptive—you meet other "family" members, etc. To me, it wouldn't mean a thing. I was never a part of that life and in my circumstances, probably wouldn't want to be—ever! Sometimes it's best to find out just a few things, and let the rest be unknown. The only time *I* would search is if I knew I had siblings, and we had been separated at an early age [emphasis in the original].[2]

---

[1]Sheila believes that her father died on the USS *Bristol* (DD-453), a destroyer which the German submarine U-371 torpedoed and sank on October 13, 1943. The *Bristol*, escorting a convoy from Salerno to Oran, was cut in two by the torpedo. For further information on the sinking, see Vol. IX, *Sicily-Salerno-Anzio, January 1943-June 1944* (Boston: Little, Brown, 1968), pp. 312–313, of Samuel Eliot Morison's *History of United States Naval Operations in World War II*. For a photograph of the *Bristol*, see Paul H. Silverstone, *U.S. Warships of World War II* (Garden City: Doubleday, 1965), p. 130.

[2]Letter from Sheila to Ann Mix, May 1995; interview with Ann Mix, April 1995; AWON information sheet; AWON. Sheila asked that her last name not be used.

(l-r) James, "George," and Sheila, November 1948 at home on Long Island, New York.

Tony:
My Father Was Very Much Alive

My mother Freda, of Essex, England, and my father, who was a Captain in the United States 4th Armored Division, were enjoying a wartime love affair when he was stationed in England prior to the Normandy invasion. In 1944 the invasion began and shortly after that event my mother sent him a letter advising him she was pregnant. She received a letter back from my father's commanding officer advising her that my father had been killed on the night of the 5th–6th of July 1944.

My mother's family was a strict middle-class family with Victorian values who would not accept her in her pregnant condition. Being unable to support me on her own she placed me in an orphanage.

I was eventually adopted by an elderly couple and endured a tough street-smart upbringing, hanging around gypsy camps and working every job I could to try and equal my peers. The words "bastard" and "adopted" were often used by my classmates at school. At sixteen years old, I headed out for Australia and after several

191

years ended up in Vietnam. Our small unit of full-time profession-
als were made part of the elite USA 173rd Airborne Brigade, a society I belong to today with pride. In 1978 my remaining adoptive
parent died, and I then asked my adoptive sister what she knew of
my natural parents.

I was living in Australia then and my sister in England. She
gave me the recorded names of both my natural parents. My mother
was listed in the London telephone directory, having never married, and was living alone. I made a telephone approach and she
was overjoyed to find me. However she was so overcome by emotion and fear that it took three trips to England before she could
greet me face to face. We are now good friends.

She told me as much as she could about my father, that he had
studied forestry management with Oregon State University and had
been working in Klamath Falls, Oregon.

In 1989, my best friend left Australia to marry a girl in St Louis,
Missouri. I flew over for the wedding. I loved America and eventually moved here after fourteen visits. I married, had a daughter, and
decided to obtain citizenship in my father's name. I was granted a
court decree as a legal son and heir of the deceased Captain in September of 1991. In 1994 (at age fifty) I wanted to apply for a USA
passport and I needed my father's birth certificate, school transcripts
and military records.

Upon checking in Klamath Falls, Oregon, I found no record of
my father. It was then I heard about the American WWII Orphans
Network and spoke to Ann Mix. She checked casualty lists and none
of the men matched what I had been told about my father. She suggested my father had not been killed in World War II and I should
search for someone who had survived the war. She suggested I try
to get my father's records from his university and high school.

I contacted the Oregon State University for my dad's records
and there was a bomb shell. The assistant registrar advised me that
my father was very much alive and sent me a directory of information and a 1941 photograph. When I contacted the high school he
went to, the business administrator turned out to be my father's

niece! She was in legless shock when asked by a mystery cousin for her uncle's education transcript.

My new-found cousin agreed to be postman and arranged a meeting with my father who is married with two grown children. He had doubts about me and stalled his niece until my mother named his commanding officer, who had dated her girl friend, described them both, and named the place where they had met. He was the only Captain in the 4th Armored Division with his name and the only one studying foresty management with Oregon State University, no mistaken identity, just facts. He had another meeting with [his] niece and read through my letters. He said I seemed like the sort of person he would like to meet and he would comply with my requests to assist with my identity. He advised her that he would tell his wife and let his niece assist with the documentation. I took it that my lifelong quest was finally being fulfilled.

But, this was not to be. After a three-week delay, my cousin rang and said that my father had rung her and told her the bets were off and that he had hired an attorney. His niece's thoughts were that by admitting to paternity his wife would be, or could be, cut out of an estate. I have since received a letter from my father's attorney to cease contact or risk a legal remedy.

My mother's feelings are indescribable. Although, if any one has the right to be angry it is me. I forgive them both. (Matthew 6:14) I have written a final plea to my father offering to waive any claim to his estate and refrain from any legal action against him. In return I want his name on my citizenship application instead of a blank space reserved for "bastards." It is the right of any orphan to fight for their identity and birthright. My fight is real and I will not give in. To turn my back on my identity is to lose the self esteem I have finally established over fifty years. Even though I have not resolved my situation with my biological father, I have achieved inner peace through discovering my perpetual father, who is always with me.[1]

Tony Harris
Branson, Missouri[2]

[1]Through evidence obtained from government documents, Tony was able to become a United States citizen. His father, however, has continued to refuse to recognize his paternity. He has asked that his father's name be kept confidential.
[2]Letter and attachment of June 8, 1994; phone interview with Ann Mix, October 9, 1997; AWON files.

Tony Harris in 1945, after being adopted by the Harris family in Bristol, England.

Freda Nethercott (on the right) and her mother. Tony received this first picture from his mother in 1978, after tracing her to London. He was living in Australia at the time, having left England at age 16.

Tony Harris (kneeling in back) in Vietnam in 1965, serving with the USA 173rd Airborne Brigade.

Tony's first meeting with his mother Freda Nethercott in 1988 at the Thames River in England. "I Tony Harris had not been with her since birth January 1945."

Cassandra Skye Harris and her proud father Tony Harris in Branson, Missouri, in October 1996.

Gloria:
I Needed to Be Somebody

*G*loria has few memories of her father, Rocco Zuccarella. She was only two years old when he enlisted in the Army. The family was from New York City, and her father had quite a reputation in the city for his gambling prowess: "I understand that we never lacked for anything. He was very successful." Her father's brother, Uncle Bill, recalls that Rocco was not drafted, but instead chose to go:

Uncle Bill just doesn't talk about my father. All he ever said to me—and now he's in his eighties and very frail—is Rocco just didn't have to go. He volunteered.

Gloria's mother did not see Rocco before the Army sent him to Europe:

My mother was working at a hotel in New York, and my father went off for his final training. His unit was put on a ship. I don't even know where he trained, but they came into New York, and they were not supposed to get off the ship. They were getting ready

197

to go to England. He knew a lot of the guys down on the docks because he was a New Yorker. He found his way off and went and saw my grandmother and evidently saw me, but my mother was not home. That was one night when she had gone out with a friend after work or something. So my mother never saw him after he had gone off for training.

Rocco saw action in France, Belgium, Holland, and into Germany. On March 5, 1945, Gloria's father, then a Staff Sergeant in the 49th Infantry Battalion, 8th Armored Division, won the Silver Star for saving members of his platoon from enemy fire. A picture of Rocco receiving his medal included this caption:

Staff Sgt. Rocko Zuckerella [Rocco Zuccarella], then private, infantry, United States Army, for gallantry in action against the enemy in Germany on 5 March 1945. Under intense enemy fire, Sgt. Zuckerella covered members of his platoon with machine gun fire while they took cover. He then advanced 800 yards under machine gun, artillery, mortar and small arms fire to lead 12 men to safety. Sgt. Zuckerella's actions reflect great credit upon himself and the Armed Forces of the United States. Entered military service from New York.

As Gloria observed, "I guess he was sort of a tough guy, with his gambling and everything, but obviously his street-smart, New York personality and everything came out when it needed to come out." One month later, German fire cut down Sgt. Zuccarella outside Werl, Germany (Werl is in the Ruhr area, east of Dortmun). Two months later the war was over in Europe.

Gloria's grandfather had a premonition of his son's death:

I can remember one recollection of my grandfather—and, see, nobody really talked much about my father's death. But my grandfather did say once that he woke up, startled, and my father was there saying, "Take care of them. Take care of them for me." And a couple of days later the telegram came.

Gloria was four years old, and her father's death brought an abrupt change to her life:

My mother sent me to Bergenfield, New Jersey, to stay with my father's sister, Aunt Phyllis, and her husband. I really don't remember my mother coming out much. I know she had to work, but I don't remember a lot of visits. And then I remember her going off to California. She had met my stepdad, who was in the Merchant Marine. She went out to California, and then all of a sudden she came back, and I was taken from my aunt and uncle, who had become my family.

For Gloria, who was then eight years old, the move away from her aunt and uncle amounted to the loss of a second family:

My Aunt Phyl had really become my surrogate mother. To the day she died, I always felt she truly understood me better than my mother. . . . They had this house in Bergenfield. That was out in the country then, so I had a yard and I had my cousin Danny and my cousin Phyllis and my cousin Ruth. . . . I went through the measles in that house. I went through the chicken pox in that house. I started school when I was living there. Aunt Phyl was the one who brought me to school. . . . It was like, "What do you mean you're taking me away from them? I don't want to go with you. I'm perfectly happy here."

We went to California, and there were some rough times. Then we came back to the East Coast. Then Mom had my brother. I was nine.

Gloria's mother did not discuss Rocco or share information with Gloria. Nor, Gloria felt, did she have her mother's full love and support within the family:

Nobody really ever talked about him. I only have two pictures of my father. One is when he received the Silver Star, and the other is of the three of us before he went [overseas]. So I really don't have much. Nobody saved any of those things. My mother didn't save things. I have only one letter that came from a man from Ohio who was in my dad's group, who knew the circumstances of his death. He had written to my mother, and that was basically the only thing she saved. My mother didn't talk about it. . . .

During the last couple of years, when I talked to my brother, I said, "You know, for some reason or other I've always felt that Mother was harder on me than you." And he said, "Yes. I never saw it then, but I can see it now."

Gloria has tried to understand the reason for her mother's feelings toward her:

I think sometimes that I was a burden. I really do. I always felt like I was a burden because I was there and I was a reminder. I think that there was probably some guilt on my mother's part, not being there when he came that last night. I don't know. I guess because I was a reminder. I reminded her of something that—well, let's face it—turned her life topsy-turvy. She was very young. She was seventeen when I was born, so she was young. My dad went off when he was nineteen, I think. So by twenty-one she was a widow. That's a heavy load. I don't know; we just never seemed to mesh. We never seemed to mesh.

Nor did the problems between Gloria and her mother end there:

When my mom and stepfather moved to Panama when I was nineteen—he got a job down there—there was also a feeling of abandonment. I didn't know what was happening to me in my earlier years, but as I look back I feel like I was abandoned then and I was abandoned—all of a sudden, here I am nineteen, and they're taking off, and what am I supposed to do? Take off to a new country? What am I supposed to do, give up college? Give up my life? And my mother made it very difficult for me. She never liked Allen [my fiancé]. In the beginning, she just really didn't like him, and that really made things very difficult because he was in the Navy. We got married when he was in the Navy, and he came out of the Navy, and they wanted us to go to Panama with them. He said, "I don't want to." He said, "If we can't make it here, then maybe we'll give it a try." And my mother always resented that because my half-sister, who is my stepfather's daughter by his first marriage, [did join them]. When her husband got out of the Coast Guard, the day after he got out they went to Panama. I guess it was [then] that my mother really lost control, and it was hard for her.

There would be one final abandonment:

Then I started to get to the point in my life that I wanted to talk to her about things, but she was in the onset of Alzheimers. Now, of course, there's no way to talk at all, because she hasn't known me for I don't know how long now, for years. . . . There are things that she could tell me that would really put things to rest.

If Gloria has felt abandoned by her mother, however, she has found in her stepfather a man of wisdom, strength, and understanding. In Gloria's own words, he is "wonderful" and "very special":

I'm going to tell you something about an incredible person. When I was sixteen, my stepfather asked me if he could adopt me. I said fine because I had lost all this connection, and I needed to be somebody. We were in the lawyer's office. The lawyer said, "And now you will be known as Gloria Katherine Burrell." And my stepdad said, "Excuse me. Let me talk to my daughter a minute." And he said, "There's no reason to drop your father's name." He's a super, super human being. So my name was Gloria Katherine Zuccarella Burrell, and that was because of him, not because of my mother.

Gloria's stepfather encouraged Gloria and her mother to visit the American cemetery at Margraten, Netherlands, where Gloria's father is buried. Gloria's mother always refused such a trip. "Her excuse was that she couldn't fly. But she did fly from Panama here and everything, but she just wouldn't go there." Finally in 1985, with the continued urging of her stepfather and husband Allen, Gloria and Allen traveled to Europe, with the understanding that they would stop at Margraten as part of their tour:

We flew to Brussels, got a car, and I said to Allen, "Yes, we'll go to Margraten. We'll do that and we'll look around. Don't worry about it. Yes, we'll get there." I had made up this itinerary. This is going to be perfect. We went to Brugge [Belgium] and then up through Holland, and we were in the north of Holland at Volendam. And there was something—I really can't explain it—inside of me. I said to Allen, "You know, I realize this wasn't planned this way." I said, "I have to get down to Margraten. I have to go." He being the way he is, said, "Fine, we'll go." And we did.

We drove all the way from Volendam and got to Maastricht, and it was early evening. We found a place to stay, and the people were very nice, and we told them we were going to Margraten and [asked] where it was from the hotel. And they said, "Oh, straight out the road. But if you go out now, the gates might be closed and there's probably nobody in the office." I had, before we went, contacted the American Battle Monuments Commission, and they told me they would escort us to the grave and everything like that. And I had these papers of where his grave was and all of that.

Well, after we ate, Allen said, "Oh, we'll ride out there and see where it is." So we rode out, and the gates were open, so we went in, and I didn't have any of the papers with me. I just didn't have it in my mind where the grave was situated or anything. It was early evening, and Allen said, "Don't worry about it. We'll be back tomorrow, and then they'll bring us to the grave." There are over 8,000 graves. "Don't worry about it. We'll find it tomorrow." He started walking off in one direction, and I can only tell you that there was a pulling. And Allen as my witness, I was pulled. I was walking this way—I just don't know, but there was something. And I stopped, and there was my father's grave. I cannot to this day believe it, but I looked up, and it was his grave. All I remember is screaming, "Allen, Allen, I found him! I found him!"

It was truly a feeling that he was waiting for me. I really do believe it. It's not as if he's on the end grave or the first row. It's K53, like in the middle of everything. It's like how in God's name would you find that? But I did. I really believe it's God's miracle. But I do believe that for all these years now he was waiting for me. There had to be some closure and peace for him. I had to get there. All of those wonderful plans I had to see this part of Holland, it didn't make any difference any more. I just had to get there. . . . The American cemeteries are just beautiful. They're breathtaking. Even now, after being there five times, I think that every time I go in, I have to catch my breath because it's so beautiful. And now I really feel like he's at rest. I think he's more at peace.

Along with their return visits to Margraten, Gloria and Allen have become close friends with the Dutch family who have adopted her father's grave and keep flowers on it. In many ways, they have become part of Gloria's family. "It's like we've known each other all our lives. It's like it was just meant to be, that somewhere God has this connection, and it was just a matter of time. They're just wonderful, wonderful people."

Gloria and Allen have also visited the German town of Werl, where Gloria's father died. The war had devastated the city, leaving little but rubble:

The only thing left standing was the church. The town, of course, has been rebuilt, and there were a lot of Americans there at that time. The main street is a walkway now. You can't drive through the main street, and you have outside cafes. And we stopped to have something, and there were American soldiers sitting next to us. I just started a conversation with them. The one fellow was involved with training, and he asked, "What are you doing here?" I told him that my father had died in this area. He replied, "You should see," and then he paused, "Maybe you shouldn't see the films of the Werl area, because we use them in training, and all there was were craters."

Bit by bit, Gloria has been able to piece together other parts of her father's life. She now has her father's personal effects and a wartime book that lists the names and addresses of the men who served with her father:

My mother did have this book, because that was her writing. These things had all disappeared, and I don't know where they were hidden. My mother evidently didn't take them. She gave them to my grandmother, and when my grandmother died, my grandfather lived for several years after that. Then when he died, my Aunt Madeline, who was my father's sister, said, "I think there's something in the house that you should have." She had a little brown bag, cloth bag, and she said, "Here, when you get a chance, maybe you should look through this." It was this book and my father's medals and his glasses and his wallet.

Gloria has also made contact with one of the men in her father's unit. In looking at the names and addresses of the men in her dad's book, she found the name of the man in Ohio who had written to her mother in 1945 telling of the circumstances of Rocco's death. In his letter of June 17, 1945, written from Czechoslovakia, 1st Sergeant William Sweeney had given these details:

About 7:00 P.M. of April 8th our company was moving up to attack the city of Werl. We got within half a mile of the city when we first ran into resistance. Our 1st Platoon of which Rocky was a member was out in front. It seems the Germans were just sitting there waiting for us, and I believe they had just about every type of gun that was ever invented. The 1st Platoon was cut off from the rest of the company. After about one hour of fighting we realized we were hopelessly outnumbered, and all men were given the order to withdraw. It was while trying to get his squad back to the rest of the company that he was hit by a shell fragment. Rocky was hit in the chest, and I know he didn't suffer any because he died immediately. I saw him about two hours later and I know you will be happy to know he wasn't mutilated at all and he just looked as if he died in his sleep. He died about 10:00 P.M. approximately half a mile from Werl, Germany.

After some hesitation, Gloria decided to try to find Sergeant Sweeney, using the old address in her dad's book:

I said to Allen one night, "I'm just going to try." When I called information, they said, "Well, not at that address, but I have another William Sweeney" at such-and-such address. And I said, "Well, would you give me that number?" I called, and he answered the phone. "Mr. Sweeney," I said, "this is going to be sort of a real kind of odd phone call, but does the name Rocky Zuccarella mean anything to you?" And there was silence, and then he replied, "Yes." I said, "That was my father." "Oh, my God," he said. So we correspond and we talk to each other three or four or five times a year.

In turn, Sweeney has contacted others in Rocco's outfit to see if they might have any photographs of Gloria's father or additional information on the circumstances of his death.

In her quest for additional knowledge of her father, Gloria continues to grapple with what being a war orphan has meant to her life and to the lives of others like her:

When I was growing up, I guess we didn't realize [what it meant]. I have realized in the last couple of years some of the voids that were there, and somehow or other I guess everybody tries to compensate for them in one way or another. Some of my traits—I guess you would call them weaknesses—are things that I have done over the years to fill those voids. People consider me a very strong person, a very independent person. But I have come to learn that some of that is because of some of the insecurities that I have had. . . . I think now— still get emotional, as you can see—some of the things have come to light, and I have been able to figure out why my personality is the way it is. . . .

Now I can talk more openly about it, and I think it's really good, rather than trying to keep it inside. I mean, my kids know everything. They think it's wonderful that I've gone to Margraten and that I feel the way I do and that you can love two people [as a father]. . . .

You know, sometimes I say to myself, I'm sorry, really sorry that it took so long [to learn about my father]. That I'm really sorry about. I shouldn't have been so independent, and that this piece of my life didn't matter. . . .

I'm really embarrassed to say this, but [as I was growing up] I was almost embarrassed [not to have my real father]. Growing up at that time—I'm sure a lot of people were in the same position— you never said anything about being adopted or this wasn't your real dad or anything. My mother and my stepdad—we were a family. Even before I was adopted, I used my stepdad's name. You know when it really came to light was when I was sixteen, and I was going to get my driver's permit, and they wouldn't accept the name Burrell because that wasn't my legal name at that point. This was some months before my stepdad legally adopted me. I had to bring my birth certificate. "What do you mean I'm not a Burrell?" It was like I had put all of that orphan status aside, because I had really lost a lot of contact with [my father's side of the family]. I really think there was some sort of resentment there, that I would have to do this now. What if anybody found out [that I was an orphan]?

Even the obvious price of war could be ignored or overlooked:

A lot of people were in the same position. But it's something that you just really did not talk about. And yet it seems to me now, when you think back, how stupid could the world be? They knew all those men died. What did the world think?[1]

[1]Interview with Susan Hadler, November 1995; newspaper clipping and letter of William Sweeney, June 17, 1945; AWON files.

Family portrait before Rocco left for the Army, circa December 1943, in New York City. Gloria Guiterrez Zuccarella, Gloria Zuccarella, and Rocco Zuccarella.

Brigadier General John M. Divine, Commanding General 8th Armed Division, congratulates S/Sgt. Rocco M. Zuccarella after presenting him with the Silver Star for Gallantry in Action on 5 March 1945.

Rocco M. Zuccarella, a young son of Italian immigrants, circa 1935 in New York City.

Gloria Zuccarella Layne's first visit to Margarten, the site of her father's burial. April 1985, with husband Allen Layne.

Kathleen:

My Father May Be in Germany Buried as a German Soldier

Kathleen never saw her father. When he shipped out for the European theater in April 1944, his wife Nancy was then barely three-weeks pregnant with their first and only child, Kathleen. In two letters to AWON, Kathleen wrote of her memories of her father and her life without him:

My father John Proudfit Eaton, Jr., was born in Portland, Oregon, on May 20, 1918. He attended school and church with animals in his pockets. He found and cared for sick, lost, and lame creatures by tucking them in his pockets to keep them warm and secure. As he grew older, he included caring for lost, sick, hungry, and homeless people. The dinner table at home included new faces a few times a week.

John was an active member of the Boy Scouts and worked very hard on projects to receive the most badges in his troop. He suffered from asthma, food and pollen allergies, teased his little sister, and attended grade school and high school in Portland. He became very good at woodworking, drawing, painting, and electronics. He was always busy working with his hands. He built cages in his backyard for the larger animals he found who needed his help.

After high school, my father worked for the railroad, and joined the Army in March of 1942, as a member of HQ, 60th Tank Destroyer Battalion, 607 Tank Destroyers, 90th Infantry Division.

My mother and father met through mutual friends in Portland, and soon married in October 23, 1942. He was twenty-four and Nancy was only nineteen. They married in the home of my father's parents.

On June 30, 1944, near Pretot, France [south of Cherbourg in the Cotentin Peninsula], my father and a sergeant were returning from a radio repair assignment to their company command post when they missed their way. They continued in the wrong direction until they ran into a German minefield where they were machine gunned by the enemy. Medical personnel and a combat patrol attempted to rescue them but were forced back. . . .

On July 25, 1944, my mother received word that her husband was missing in action. She was home alone when she received the telegram.

My mother and my grandparents wrote letter after letter, made phone call after call to the U.S. Army War Department, trying to find out anything they could about my father, his disappearance, and when he would be coming home. The answers were always the same: John had been taken prisoner, and he was missing.

As the war came to a close, my mother and grandparents became very, very excited. Every day they thought the next day would surely bring good news of their husband and son, and his safe return home.

It was not until May 14, 1945, that German war records disclosed that my father was already dead. He had been dead for twenty-one days when my mother received the telegram notifying her that he was missing. They had spent the next ten months looking for him and waiting for him to come home, but he was already dead. My grandparents never ever got over the death of their only son. My grandmother never really laughed again.

According to Army records I have received, my father was wounded and taken prisoner on June 30, 1944. He died of wounds three days later on July 3, 1944. His left lower leg was broken by a bullet; he also had a wound in his lower right leg and a skull fracture. . . .

A barn belonging to the local mayor and a school were used by the Germans as an aid station during the hostilities. The mayor recalled one American soldier died in his barn on or about July 3, 1944, after midnight. The soldier had a broken leg and other wounds and was receiving good care from a German doctor. German soldiers were making burials without help from the civilians and all deceased were supposed to have been buried in the local cemeteries.

Another American soldier died of abdominal wounds. The caretakers at the local cemetery recalled that one of the Americans had been buried separately but could not state how many American[s] were buried and did not know if any Americans had been buried among the German dead.

In November of 1953 an investigation was conducted at Gerville, France. It was learned that the Americans had disinterred and removed some remains from the cemetery and at a later date approximately thirty German deceased were disinterred and reburied in a German military cemetery, among which were seven unknowns. It is believed that my father may have been one of the seven unknowns. The Army made several investigations into the graves of all the unknown soldiers for several years. In the thirty graves, twenty-four contained the major portions of individual remains with some intermingling of skeletal portions. Twenty-three of these had complete skulls with teeth, which eliminated my father. The twenty-fourth and last remains of that group had a complete skull with the maxilla area completely broken away. So that was not my father. He may be in Germany buried as a German soldier, or still in France in a makeshift graveyard or mixed in with other dead somewhere else.

My father did receive two Purple Hearts, both of which I have along with a flag that covered a coffin used to bury his unknown unbody in an ungrave. . . . Army records show my father as 5 ft. and

6 and 3/4 inches tall, weighing 134 pounds, medium frame, blue eyes, light hair, and had a shoe size of 7 and 1/2-E. He had no fractures and/or breaks shown, and no tattoos and/or birthmarks shown. His charts do show, however, that he had full upper and lower dentures given to him by the Army over a period of two years!

I inherited my father's poor teeth, shortness, poor direction, and at one time I had a medium frame. I have light eyes and small feet; a few of his allergies; love of animals and have too many at any given time; have been known (in my younger years) to bring home to dinner and/or marry the sad, rejected, and troubled misfits. I am happiest when I can draw, paint, and build things with my hands. . . .

As a child, I would fall asleep nights crying and praying for God to send my father home. I prayed that by some miracle he was not dead but just lost and that he would find his way back home to me. I made up stories about my father, about how he and I would draw together, go for walks and drives, spend Christmas together, and go to church. I would fall asleep on his lap as he read me stories; he would teach me to dance and to drive a car. I was sure that after he came home he and my mother would have more children, and I would have brothers and sisters. He would be my protector, nothing bad would ever happen to me again, he would be my best friend, he would always be on my side, he would be very smart and help me with my homework, he would give me away at my wedding, and he would be there for the birth of my children. . . .

In 1995, I received a copy of movies of my father taken in 1942. He came home from the Army on leave to marry my mother. I saw his easy smile, the way he moved his head as he spoke, his smooth walk, his gentleness and affection with my mother, his respect for his parents, and his clean, handsome looks. I was proud of him in his uniform and proud to be his daughter. . . .

My father never knew me. But I am luckier than most: He knew I was going to be born, and he and my mother loved each other only as young newlyweds can. I have wonderful photos of him and stories about him. And his sister's daughter, my cousin, is like a third best friend and sister.

My father's best Army friend, also from Oregon, came home after the war and married my mom in 1946. They gave me two sisters. I am luckier than most.

But sometimes before I fall asleep, or on his birthday, Father's Day, or a holiday, I ache for him. I want to hear his voice, smell his after shave, watch him eat, write a letter, shave, comb his hair, and to hold me. Growing up, I could feel him close to me, like a guardian angel. I would talk to him in my head and feel lucky I had two fathers. I think about him every day, and still I feel he guards me.[1]

[1]Letter of September 20, 1996; undated letter; AWON files.

Private John Proudfit Eaton, U.S. Army Hq. Co. 607 TD., 90th Div., age 24, and Nancy Jane Jones Eaton, age 19, on their wedding day, 23 October 1942, in Portland, Oregon. John was the only son of John Page Eaton and Zella Alice Proudfit Eaton. He died 3 July 1944 as a POW. His body was never recovered.

Mrs. Nancy Jones Eaton, age 22, and her daughter Kathleen May Eaton, age 2 months, in February 1945 in Portland, Oregon.

Susan:

I Raise My Glass to You,
Dear Papa, Fire and Spirit!

Susan's father, David S. Johnson, Jr.,served with the 782d Tank Destroyer Battalion and died on April 12, 1945, when he tripped a booby-trapped German anti-tank mine. He was twenty-five, an only child, and the father of David (III), age three and a half, and Susan, age three months. As a child, Susan prized pictures of her father and the letter he wrote welcoming her into the family.

I am six years old. There are several photographs in a white cardboard box beneath the family album. I love to look at the one of the two of them together. He is smiling at my mother who is facing him. His soldier's cap lies jauntily on the back of his head, one hand is in the pocket of the trousers. Only their eyes are touching. Once upon a time, he was alive and my mother and father were in love. They were married and they had a child, my brother David. Then he left for war.

One month after I was born, my father wrote me a letter of welcome. The small square photo-copied V-Mail letter is scotch taped into my baby book. Crawling behind the upholstered living room chair, I open the cabinet and fish out my baby book from underneath the stack of albums and boxes of old photos. The cover is pink with the title, "Our Baby's First Seven Years," printed in gold. First comes the picture of the hospital where I was born. Next the height and weight of my infant self are recorded in my mother's familiar slanted script. Now I am close. I turn the page and there is the letter on the bottom left hand page. Birthday cards shift around through the pages. The letter from my father is always in the same place:

Dear Susan,

Since I can't be there in person, this is a sort of "welcome" letter. Yours is a pretty good family as families run. Your dad is a bit on the off-side, but your mother and brother and now you, more than make up for that.

Your brother is quite a guy—of course, he's quite handsome and smart—will he get around—but I know he'll always be ready to guide you and protect you in every way.

Your mother is the most wonderful person I've ever known. I've always marveled at my great good fortune to have loved her and been loved by her. If you will follow her dictates and examples, you may expect to meet life in the best possible way and your path will always be the right one.

Your family believes in living life to its fullest. We enjoy all good things, and live well—in that you're fortunate.

For me, adhere to a belief in tolerance, a genuine liking for others, and always give to life to the fullest.

Your father,
Dave

Black words on white paper, the words are my father. They are his voice and his fatherly guidance. The words prove that I have a father and that he knew I was born. He tells me that he loved my mother and my brother and now me. The letter is my blessing. From his words I forge a loyalty and a love for my father.

I want to sit beside people who knew my father and listen to them talk about him. Knowing almost nothing about him, I long for stories that will bring my father to life. Stories that set my imagination to work. I can do the rest, add the colors, the expressions, the walk, the action.

I know only one story about my father. It is the story of his death. A six-year-old with freshly cut bangs, I have come to visit my grandmother, my father's mother. My tall white-haired Granny meets me at the train station and drives us across town to her apartment. Granny treats me like a grown-up, serving us dinner on trays in the living room. The china is thin, bordered with a delicate purple and gold pattern. The silver is heavy. Fragile and heavy-hearted is my dear Granny. She is talking about my father, her only child. "David and his two friends were out in the fields, making sure the way was safe for the others to follow. The area had been cleared, but your father and the other two men wanted to go first, just to make sure. All of a sudden there was an explosion. All three of them were killed." Granny is looking down, stroking one thin hand with the other. I long to put my head in her lap. There are no words. We do not touch. There is nothing else in life; only this godforsaken silence. An uncrossable barrier surrounds my grandmother and now me.

The story of my father's death is as much a part of me as my eyes, the way I "see" my father. He is brave and good. I see him in his uniform with his friends, one on each side of him. They are talking and joking, walking along together in a golden field under a blue sky. Then BOOM! The explosion. I see red and yellow fire and bits of the black earth and my father thrown up into the sky. That's where the story ends. There are no more stories. Only nightmares.

I have no name for him. Granny calls my father "Daddy David." She is trying to share him with me. But he is hers. She knew him all his life. "Daddy David" is awkward. "Daddy" is endearing and familiar. I don't know him. "David" is my brother's name. I don't know where my father fits in my life. I don't know how to see him or how to relate to him.

Church hymns are the only place that mention "my father." I stand tall and sing out in my off key voice, ". . . land where our fathers died. . . ." My father is like the "Almighty Father" in the hymn "God of our Fathers in whose almighty hands leads forth in beauty all the starry bands. . . ." I sing with silent knowledge and devotion, "This is my father's world. . . ." I pray fervently to "Our Father who art in heaven." At these holy moments the dead and the living merge and I belong.

November 11. Veteran's Day. Every year I stand with the rest of my class for two minutes of silence. One yearly moment when soldiers like my soldier father are remembered by everyone at the same time. I tell no one my secret, but I know that the silence means death; soldiers, men being shot and blown up, their lives over as quickly as the two minutes elapse. We go on living and the soldiers and my father never do. I want the silence to last for a long time and then I want to tell my friends and my teachers about my father. I secretly want people to know that my father is one of the soldiers we were remembering. I want them to know I am connected to my hero father. I want someone to touch me on the shoulder and say, "I'm sorry your father was killed." Then I could say, "Oh, it's alright, but thanks." I can be sort of a hero, like my father. But I will never tell. What if people have nothing to say? How pathetic I would feel, needing comfort, attention, and getting none. Or they might tell me that he was a soldier and soldiers die or that I should be proud of my father who "gave" his life. Then I would feel ashamed of myself for wanting someone to recognize our loss. I keep my secret safe and private.

As a child, Susan kept her questions and thoughts about her father to herself. With adulthood, she could no longer stifle her desire to learn of her father. Within her family, however, she was alone in her quest. Her mother had remarried, and Susan now had five half-brothers and -sisters.

I sequestered my longing to know about my father until I grew older and left my parents' house. My longing to know my father spewed out like lava from a volcano. I could no longer keep my desire to know inside of me. My grandmother was dead [she had committed suicide when Susan was seventeen] and could never answer my questions.

My mother was the only one I knew who knew him. And she would not answer my questions. We fought over the past. My mother believed the past belonged to her. She fought to keep the past for herself. My father was her past. It belonged to her. I fought to acquire the past. My father was my past. It belonged to me, and I needed her help to know my father and claim my legacy. She told me that she didn't want to remember that painful period of her life. She had put it behind her and I should do the same. The rest of the family encircled my mother protectively. I was outside of that circle, seen as the one who upset our mother. I felt guilty. I didn't want to hurt my mother. I was angry. I wanted to know who my father was. I took courage from Antigone who risked her life to remember her brother slain in battle.

When Susan finally pried open her mother's silence, she found that there was nothing there; her mother had little to say or knowledge to give. Her quest had been for naught.

My mother sat across the table from me in the hotel dining room and told me that she did not remember my father very well. She had known him for only five years. They were young and the war imposed itself on every aspect of their life together. She didn't remember him, he who was a god to me, a mysterious source of life and love. She didn't really remember very much about him. She could not remember the things I needed to know about him so that I could transform my unknown god-soldier-hero into a father I could know and remember. At that moment I did not know my mother, this woman who bore me and forgot my father. The mother I imagined did not exist. I was alone.

Susan's emotional solitude lasted until Veterans Day, 1992, when a visit to the Vietnam Memorial made her determined to renew her search for her father.

The morning after I went to the Wall, I looked up a vet center in the phone book. I felt eager and pathetic, pathetic that I was nearly fifty years old and so unresolved and needy and isolated as to look in a damned phone book for someone to talk to about an event that happened half a century ago. I was afraid they would tell me it was the wrong war, I was too old or too late.

A man with a voice like a cello answered the phone. He was kind when I told him that my father had been killed in World War II and that I wanted to begin to know and grieve him. That blessed man accepted my need and my longing. "When it hits, it hits hard."

Now began an odyssey that would take Susan ultimately to the still-pockmarked soil where her father died. She obtained his military service records. "Within two minutes I knew more facts about my father than I have ever known." Included was the notation that her father had died in Mechernich, Germany, southeast of Aachen, as well as a 1949 document from the American Graves Registration Command which noted:

From the facts herein presented it can only be concluded that 2nd Lt. David S. Johnson, Jr., was killed in the action mentioned above and that his remains were completely disintegrated by the explosion of the mine, thus precluding recovery. This conclusion can be further substantiated by the fact that the remains of (the other man killed) were mutilated and the remains of (the other man killed) consisted of the left leg only, and after the incident no remains of Lt. Johnson could be found.

There was also a copy of a final letter sent to Susan's mother in January 1951:

Several years have elapsed since the cessation of hostilities of World War II, which cost the life of your husband, the late Second Lieutenant David S. Johnson, Jr.

It is with deep regret that your Government finds it necessary to inform you that further search and investigation have failed to reveal the whereabouts of your husband's remains. Since all efforts to recover and/or identify his remains have failed, it has been necessary to declare that his remains are not recoverable.

Realizing the extent of your great loss, it is with reluctance that you are sent information that there is no grave at which to pay homage. May the knowledge of your husband's honorable service to his country be a source of sustaining comfort to you.

Armed with her newly found knowledge and haunted by the phrase "there is no grave at which to pay homage," Susan began searching out members of her father's unit, devouring and savoring every piece of knowledge they could share. With their help and understanding, the shape and character of her father's life emerged, even if imperfectly. In the midsummer of 1994, she and her husband retraced her father's movements across Europe, from his arrival at Le Havre, to his first encampment at St. Valery en Caux in France, to his death just inside the German border. In Luxembourg, she stopped at the American Cemetery, where her father's name is carved on the wall of the missing.

The cemetery at first seems to emphasize the military and "sacrifice." Neither of those aspects touches me. My reaction is to pull back inside myself. I have just begun to know my father. I don't want to leave the personal time I have finally had with him and return to the collective, to the sense of him as myth, an impersonal fallen soldier, one of millions of fallen soldiers. I felt the power of that myth as a child when I longed to touch my once human father and ran into the cold stone statue of the warrior hero. Society, teachers, ministers, talked about World War II in a way that left me feeling that my father's death was something good, something "sacrificial," something godlike. I was confused. Death was sad. It was lonely. It was scary. Death meant my father wasn't with me. When I began to feel my loss, I would feel guilty and unable to trust my pain. I felt empty and lost because my father died. Yet his death meant others lived, so how could I be so selfish as to complain or speak of my own loss and hurt? I didn't speak of it. As I grew, I identified with Jews for whom the war meant murder, death and loss. I read the literature of the Holocaust and felt the anguish and strength of the survivors before I knew my own. Their courage to write of what they experienced gave me courage. I have begun to speak of my father, his life and his death as part of my history, as part of myself. I don't want my father to be forgotten, nor do I want his memory to be exploited.

As I walk away from the wall, I look back and see a group of people gathering at the place where I left flowers. A few flowers, a gift of loss and love and remembrance softening the impersonal uniformity of the five thousand dead who are buried here. People stop. A few will read his name.[1]

On the road between Mechernich and Euskirchen, Susan found the place of her father's death. Along an old neglected path through a grove of trees, she saw the crater carved by the mine. Jagged blocks of concrete lay on the side of the path silently testifying to the force of the explosion. From the bottom of the crater, younger trees had grown, while the older trees remain entangled and deformed with the strands of barbed wire strung half a century before.

I came to life as you went to death,
my eager reckless Papa.

It has taken me fifty years to find you
after you were blown to bits in the war.

I found you in a tiny French village
in a room at the top of the stairs.

I found you in your camp on the coast of France
sharing your whiskey with your men.

I found you in Aachen
as I entered the valley of the shadow of your death.

I found the "wooded section."
I found the crater made by the bomb that ripped open the
     earth and you.

The earth is still carved out,
but it's covered now with ferns that ripple in the wind.

Barbed wire that marked the spot fifty years ago
enters at the centers of the trees.

I sat down on that holy ground
and I talked with you there.

You would be seventy-five years old today.
I raise my glass to you, dear Papa, fire and spirit!

[1]Susan Hadler wrote this as part of a personal memoir in 1995; AWON files.

A family portrait taken in Oshkosh, Wisconsin, in 1941. Clockwise from top: David S. Johnson, Jr., Loretta Meyer Johnson, David S. Johnson, III, Lulu Meyer. All four generations lived in the same house.

David S. Johnson, Jr., with his father, David S. Johnson, Sr. Lake Winnebago, Oshkosh, Wisconsin, circa 1938.

Margery Laughlin Johnson with son David (on right) and daughter Susan Laughlin Johnson. Photo was taken in March 1945 to send to Lieutenant Johnson in France. The family is unsure whether or not he received it before being killed by a land mine in Germany on 12 April 1945.

Lieutenant David S. Johnson, Jr., at Camp Lucky Strike, St. Valery en Caux, France, Winter 1945.

Appendix

Searching for Fathers Who Died in World War II

*O*n March 1, 1987, when my mother died, I was forty-seven years old. On the same day I was given a box which contained my father's effects, sent to my mother when he was killed in World War II. It was a small cardboard box worn smooth with dirt and age. Unaware of what was in it, I pulled off the lid and found my father rushing back from the dead to meet me. The most personal things my father owned were in that box: his pen, his razor, his soap dish, his lighter, his pipe (strapped with tape where the stem had come undone). Instinctively I raised this to my nose and sniffed. The pipe still smelled of his tobacco after over forty years! My tears came like an ocean flooding out of me. How well I remembered everything that I now held in my lap. It was as if my dad had just walked into the room, whistling and cracking jokes, one more time.

This little box of my father's things, coming in the wake of my mother's death, made me sad and made me angry. Where had this box been? Why had it taken forty years for me to be given these things?

Along with sadness over losing the father I barely knew, I felt anger and loneliness at the silence surrounding him which had been such a huge part of my life. I wanted to know who he really was and how he died. I wanted to get to know him beyond the fact that I was told he was a hero who died for freedom.

I began my effort to rehumanize my father. I sent for records, talked to people and began to be able to see a dim picture of who he was. As I learned more about him, he became more real to me. Since then I have tried to get as much information about my father, his life and his death as I possibly could. I wanted to put flesh on his bones. As painful as learning the truth was, it also set me free from the bondage of fifty years of unanswered questions and silence.

I have since learned most war orphans and other family members knew almost nothing about those who died. Rarely did we know where they served, or where and how they were killed. We also knew almost nothing about them as civilians, with lives outside the war. If you ask war orphans for a photo of their father, they will inevitably pull out one of a young man in uniform. Our fathers, forever young, were mythologized into heroes by the society in which we lived, by our mothers and by ourselves. *Records*, and the information they contain, are the key to making our fathers human again.

Records have given me the great gift of insight and, in some cases, restored memories which I had lost. For the last several years I have been digging up the bones of my father's life. I have learned more about him than I ever heard from my family. I now know he dropped out of high school and he was getting bad grades. I had always thought he was a genius, and maybe he was, but he didn't like school. His favorite classes seemed to be photography and saxophone. Only when I read his high school records did I *remember* he played the saxophone. Memories of my dad and his sax came flooding back to me, precious memories I want to keep. I feel closer to my dad now than ever before.

You will too if you search.

The quality and quantity of records increased with time during World War II. They are scarce for 1942 but get much better by

1945. Some records, such as special orders and most rosters, were destroyed. For general histories of World War II and other American conflicts, see Robin Higham, ed. *A Guide to the Sources of United States Military History* (Hamden, CT: Archon Books, 1975). This volume not only contains bibliographical essays by well-known military historians, but also includes discussion of relevant government, museum, and archival sources. The editor has tried to update the volume every five years. Higham's volumes provide an excellent starting place for anyone wanting to learn more about World War II or wondering where to begin research on that conflict.

For general information the **U.S. Army Military History Institute** is very helpful. They have many bibliographies on their holdings and on specific units of the army as well as the official historical series published by the Army, Marine Corps, Army Air Force and Navy after World War II. Their primary focus is on the Army, and they receive materials from Army libraries as well as from individual donors. Original souce materials are a vital part of the Institute's holdings: diaries, letters, memoirs, photographs, art work, and personal records of prominent generals and thousands of junior officers and enlisted men and women whose service contributed to American military history from the colonial period to the present. Contact:

U. S. Army Military History Institute
Carlisle Barracks, Bldg. 22
Carlisle PA 17013-5008
Phone: (717) 245-3611

Once you have collected the necessary background information and are ready to begin your records search on a specific veteran, you will need photocopies of documents proving your relationship to the veteran. Make sure you have a copy of your birth certificate, and try to get a copy of your veteran's marriage certificate.

The first record you should send for is the record from the **Department of Veterans Affairs (VA)**. This record will have the veteran's service number in it and also may have a social security number. It will show designated next of kin and will contain marriage records and birth certificates. To get these records call (800) 827-1000, which will ring at your regional office. They will be able to tell you where your veteran's records are. Write to that address, requesting a complete copy of everything in their file, and enclosing copies of your birth certificate. (Remember you are only eligible for these records if you are next of kin and the veteran was killed or missing in action.)

If you *already have* the selective service number, you will want to write to the **National Personnel Records Center (NPRC)** for the veteran's "jacket." Ask for a copy of everything they have in your veteran's personnel records, including the "MED" records. (You must have a selective service number and ask for "MED" records specifically, as they are only filed under the selective service number. These are not filed by name). Additionally, you can apply for any medals which you lost or never received. Write to:

National Personnel Records Center
Military Personnel Records
9700 Page Boulevard
St. Louis MO 63132

The NPRC also maintains daily morning reports for the period 1917–1974 for every company in the Army, telling where the soldiers are, listing casualties and people coming and going, and even describing the weather. Ask for morning reports from the date your veteran would have entered that outfit until a few days after he died. Be specific about what unit he was with (example: 5th Army, 10th Mt. Division, 87th Mt. Infantry, Company A) and where they were fighting (Italy). It takes at least three months to get these records. The specific contact person within the National Personnel Records Center (at the same address as above) is:

Chief, Army Reference Branch NCPMA-O
Military Personnel Records

It takes a long time to get these records so the sooner you request them the better. Also, be aware that many of these records were burned in a fire at the center in 1973, but they will at least send proof of service. If you get lucky there will be much more.

Next, write for the mortuary records, which are especially useful if the personnel records were burned. These records were created to document the disposition of remains or to document the investigation into why there were no remains. They have important information in them even if no body was recovered, including the sending of personal effects to the next of kin. All mortuary records for World War II, for all branches, are kept at the **Total Army Personnel Command (TAPC)**. These are called the "Individual Deceased Personnel Files" (IDPF). Contact:

Army Commander
U. S. Total Army Personnel Command
ATTN: TAPC-PED-F
Alexandria VA 22331-0482
Phone: (703) 325-5300 Fax: (703)-325-5315

In addition, the Navy's **Mortuary Affairs Branch** has index cards on deceased sailors which relate to the remains and include a description of how the seaman was killed. Write to:

Officer In Charge
Naval Medical and Dental Affairs
Mortuary Affairs Branch
PO Box 886999
Great Lakes IL 60088-6999
Phone: (800) 876-1131 ex 621, 627, or 628 Fax: (847) 688-3964

The **Marine Corps Commandant** has copies of death certificates on microfilm. To have them send you a copy, contact:

Marine Corps Commandant
Code M-HP-10
Hdqtrs Marine Corps
2 Navy Annex
Washington DC 20380-1775
Phone: (703) 696-1177 Fax: (703) 696-2072

While you are waiting for answers to these queries, go to your local library and get books about World War II and books on your veteran's outfit. Check the library archives for possible letters, oral histories, or journals from other veterans. Check your state archives also. Become knowledgeable about the war and where your veteran fought. Study maps and brush up on your geography. Doing this makes it easier for others to talk to you, and it makes it easier to know where to look for information.

The **National Archives** is a depository of the permanently valuable, non-current records of the Federal Government. The mission of the Archives is to preserve records and make them available to the public. They have unit records, historical reports, after-action reports, journals (kept by Command) of month-to-month narratives, crime records, and general orders, including descriptions of what some unit members did to get an award. They also have station lists, including foreign lists, which tell what outfits were stationed in what area on a certain date. The files are arranged by unit. Identification of the division and regiment is necessary before a search can be conducted. These files *do not* include personnel or medical information. The archivist will research records and send photocopies of index cards.

The National Archives also stores photographs taken by United States government employees, either military or civilian, during World War II. Photos taken while the photographer was working in an official capacity are considered to be in the public domain. Permission is not required to use these items. The National Archives also has photographs taken by private citizens or by organizations other than the United States government, but many of these are subject to copyright laws.

Army Air Force unit combat mission reports for World War II are also stored at the National Archives. These consist of the original mission reports pertaining to specific targets, as filed by the units, and they include some encounter reports by pilots, some aerial photographs, and some loading lists. These reports are arranged by units, and identification of the group or squadron is necessary before a search can be conducted.

The National Archives also keeps missing aircrew reports (MACR, Record Group 92), starting in late May of 1943 when the Army Air Forces required that a report be filed when a crew was lost in combat. During the course of World War II some 16,700 of these reports were filed. There are three indices to the report: one by name of individual crew member, one by date of loss, and one by plane tail number. If the fate of the crew was established within a few days, a report often was not filed.

These reports are available on microfiche, but if you do not have a fiche reader you can take them to your local library to view and make copies.

Another type of record at the National Archives is the "ship's deck log," a brief record of the internal administrative and mechanical workings of the ship. When the ship is underway, the log records such information as the ship's location, course and speed, sea and weather conditions, information relating to the ship's machinery, and any unusual events. When the ship is in port, a record is kept of arrivals and departures of individuals. Normally, a deck log contains little information regarding the mission on which the ship is involved. It is not a detailed journal describing all the events transpiring in and around the ship. If the ship was sunk, the log most likely went down with it and would not be available, but there would be a command ship or another ship that would have a log and might report the sinking of the ship. All ship's rosters through 1967 are held by the National Archives on microfilm. Call or write for a request form NATF81. Fill out the form, send it back, and they will search. If a roster is found there will be a charge of $10 for a copy, but there is no charge if no roster is located. These rosters are of officers only; enlisted men would be on muster rolls.

For any of the records above contact:

The National Archives At College Park
Archives II Textual Reference Branch NNR2
8601 Adelphi Rd
College Park MD 20740-6001
Phone: (301) 713-7250 Fax: (301) 713-7482

The holdings of the **Air Force Historical Research Agency (AFHRA)** consist of nearly 60,000,000 pages devoted to the history of the service. It is the largest and most valuable organized collection of documents on U.S. Military aviation. Some documents are classified or restricted, but many are open to the public. The collection includes unit histories of various Air Force organizations and documentation gathered since 1942, historical monographs and studies, oral history interviews, end-of-tour reports, personal papers, and miscellaneous documents of various organizations including the Army, British Air Ministry and German Air Force. They have USAF individual aircraft record cards and a large collection of material relating to USAF activities in the War in Southeast Asia. General descriptions of the Agency's holdings may be found in the National Union Catalog of Manuscript Collections, various library directories and other published works. A number of other detailed finding aids are also available at the center. Of particular interest are records on Air Force members who were killed or missing in action. They also have mission reports from World War II and unit histories and rosters. Check here if your veteran served in the Army Air Force. The material here differs from that at the National Archives II, in that unit reports—including mission reports pertaining to specific targets—are filed by unit and include reports by pilots, aerial photographs and loading lists. Knowledge of the group and/or squadron is necessary to make a search.

AFHRA also has military intelligence photo interpretation records (MIPI's) for World War II. For these you need the date of the mission and the target (city and country). Useful to some orphans are the German records seized by the United States during World War II, which may contain accounts of American aircraft downed and the fate of their crews (Record Group 242). These records should be used in conjunction with the missing air crew reports at National Archives II.

Army Air Force accident reports were released for research by AFHRA for the first time in March 1995. These relate to planes and aircrew who were lost as a result of accidents prior to 1956, so they include World War II and Korea (except for Marine or Naval Air). These microfilmed reports differ from missing air crew reports in that they could be records of state-side accidents or any accident involving Army Air Force planes. They will research and copy information on a crew if you provide the date and location and any other information you already know. Responses will take at least five months, and faxing or e-mailing your request will not speed up the response time.

For all records mentioned above contact the Air Force Research Agency at:

Air Force Historical Research Agency
Historical Research Center
AFHRA-RS
600 Chennault Circle
Maxwell Air Force Base AL 36112-6424
Phone: (334) 953-2437 Fax: (334) 953-4096

The Center's collection is also recorded on microfilm, with copies available at other agencies. To order copies of microfilm contact AFHRA or:

The National Archives At College Park
Archives II Textual Reference Branch NNR2
8601 Adelphi Rd
College Park MD 20740-6001
Phone: (301) 713-7250 Fax: (301) 713-7482

Air Force History Support
500 Duncan Ave Box 94
Bolling Air Force Base
Washington DC 20336-1111
Phone: (202) 404-2182 or 2179 Fax: (202) 404-2271

The **Naval Historical Center** publishes histories of ships, a dictionary of Naval Fighting Ships and general information. You can contact them for a catalog. They can also help guide you to other sources on the history of ships. Contact:

Ships' Histories Branch Naval Historical Center
901 M St SE
Washington DC 20374-5060
Phone: (202) 433-3643 Fax: (202) 433-6677

A ship's muster roll lists name, pay rate, and the date when individuals came on board. Check with the **Military Service Branch of the National Archives and Records Service** for current prices of copies of microfilm. To get a duplicate sixteen mm positive microfilm copy of your veteran's ship's muster roll contact:

Military Service Branch (Nnrm)
National Archives and Records Service
General Services Administration
Washington DC 20408

To get a hard copy of each page of your veteran's ship's muster roll you can write to the National Personnel Records Center (described on pages 228–29.) There is a charge for this. Contact:

The National Personnel Records Center
Military Personnel Records
9700 Page Ave
St Louis MO 63132

To get a copy of a photo of your veteran's ship, send to either of the addresses below; give the ship's number and/or name. They will let you know if they have a photo and the cost of a duplicate:

Still Picture Branch
The National Archives at College Park
8601 Adelphi Rd
College Park MD 20740-6001

U.S. Naval Institute
2062 Generals Hwy
Annapolis MD 21402
Phone: (800) 233-8764 or phone: (410) 268-6110
Fax: (410) 269-7940

The **American Battle Monuments Commission** is in charge of the burial sites of the 134,548 American servicemen in American military cemeteries overseas. Over 78,000 servicemen whose remains were not recovered are listed on the Tablets of the Missing located at these cemeteries and on East Coast and West Coast Memorials in the United States. The commission will send you a brochure and the exact location of your veteran's grave or listing on the Tablet of the Missing. They will also send, if you request it, a photograph of the cemetery with a photo of the veteran's marker, or a photo of his name on the Tablet of the Missing, superimposed. For a small fee they will put flowers on the grave or near a name on the Tablet of the Missing. If you do not have a service number, they may supply that also.

When traveling overseas, primarily to visit the place of burial or a memorial, immediate members of the family (widows, parents, children, sisters, brothers and guardians) will be eligible for a "Non-fee" or "Fee-free" Passport. Apply to the address below for eligibility. This commission has records of all those who are buried in American overseas cemeteries or whose names are engraved on the Tablets of the Missing. Requests for information and photographs should be addressed to the Commission in Washington, DC. Contact:

American Battle Monuments Commission Operations
Court House Plaza 2 Suite 500
2300 Clarendon Blvd
Arlington VA 22201
Phone: (703) 696-6897 Fax: (703) 696-6666

When you have exhausted local libraries and archives, branch out to national sources. An excellent list of military base libraries across the country is contained in the book *How to Locate Anyone Who Is or Has Been in the Military* by Lt. Col. Johnson (Spartanburg, SC: MIE Publishing, n.d.). Get in the habit of going to libraries and museums when you travel. What you will find will surprise and enlighten you.

After you know more about the war and about the outfit in which your veteran fought, you are ready to find a reunion of his outfit and attend it. Take a camera and a tape recorder. You don't want to miss anything someone might tell you about your veteran's service. You can also write a letter to the newsletter of the veteran's outfit. They will probably publish it, and many times men respond with information.

To find a contact for a veterans World War II outfit you can try calling the **American Legion VETS Operating Center**. The charge is currently $1.95 per minute, and it takes about two minutes to do a search. Part of the proceeds go to the American Legion. This is not for locating individuals, *only reunions*. Phone: (900) 737-8387.

Try tracking down your veteran's school records. See if his school is having a reunion or has an alumni association. Attend a reunion. Put an ad in their newsletter. Try to find his school friends. Many colleges and universities published honor rolls of those who died who had attended their school, or mentioned them in newsletters. Often these publications include photos. Check the alumni association library or college or high school library even if the veteran did not graduate.

Ask the local paper of your veteran's hometown to print a notice that says you are looking for people who knew him. Some newspapers will publish a notice like this free of charge or they will publish a letter to the editor. Others will require you to run a paid ad.

Many employers published newsletters during the war and kept others updated on the employees who were "over there." Check with your library for any publication by that company, or contact the company archivist. For example Firestone Tires and McCann Shoes both had publications which mentioned men who were serving, those who were killed, and news of their families.

Talk to relatives. Talk to people who married into the family. Talk to neighbors. Whenever you talk to anyone about your veteran, take good notes, or use a tape recorder. You may think you will remember what is discussed, but chances are you will not remember everything.

Take photographs of important documents, and make copies of photographs in the possession of others. You can flatten the photo with a piece of dull, but clear, Plexiglass to prevent glare. Use a tripod or balance the camera. It is best if you don't have to use a flash. Also, color copiers make better copies of black and white photos. Give someone else a copy of everything you gather in case there is a natural disaster or fire. This will make the other person happy *and* protect this valuable history. Protect the photos to pass them on to generations to come. In this way we keep the memory of our departed soldiers, sailors and airmen alive.

The advice given in this appendix will help you begin your journey, but more indepth information about finding records and benefits is available in my book: *Touchstones: A Guide to Records, Rights and Resources for the Next of Kin of American WWII Casualties*, by Ann Bennett Mix, AGLL Publishing. This can be ordered from:

The AWON Book Store
PO Box 4369
Bellingham WA 98227
$19.95 plus $3.00 postage

Also, the American WWII Orphans network publishes a quarterly newsletter which is a benefit of the $25 annual membership. We have located over 1,000 children of men who were killed and missing in action. We are trying to find and register every one we can. Registration is free. If you are a war orphan, or know of one, we would appreciate your letting us know. We would like to hear from other relatives also.

AWON has local gatherings around the country, and a national conference every two years to which we invite all family members and others who are interested.

For more information about *Touchstones*, about the war orphans network, or to check to see if we have someone listed who you are trying to locate, please write:

American WWII Orphans Network
PO Box 4369
Bellingham WA 98227
Phone: (360) 733-1678 Fax (360) 715-8180
E-mail awon@aol.com

Sources which may be useful to families who lost members in other wars:

Vietnam:
Sons and Daughters in Touch
PO Box 1596
Arlington, VA 22201
800 984 9994
Email: EGKH35@prodigy.com

Korean War:
Korean / Cold War Family Association of the Missing
128 Beaver Run Dr
Coppell, TX 75019-4849

POWs and Missing in Action:
Ex-Prisoners of War
3201 E Pioneer PKWY #40
Arlington, TX 76010-5396

Defence POW / MIA Office
2400 Defence Pentagon
Washington DC 20301-2400

Acknowledgments

Eternal thanks to you who have told us your stories and given us the strength to seek and to mourn our fathers and yours. Thank you my friends and collegues who encourage, listen, engage and understand what this work means to me: Ellen Baker, Julie Bondanza, Margot Born, Vikki Bravo, Mollie Donovan, Nick Etcheverry, Suzanne Goldberg, Alice Berliner Hadler, Rochelle Kainer, Linda Miller, Anna Sofaer, Carol Taliaferro, Laura Tracy, Henny Wenkart, and Frank Winford.

A special thank you to my family: Jacques and Kim for sustaining me with good food and love, and most of all to Sarah and Jack who made it possible. Rita Leahy so personably transcribed the interviews. We are deeply indebted to Cal Christman who has helped us tell the stories with matchless clarity and sensitivity. It has been our good fortune to find Fran Vick and Charlotte Wright and the UNT Press. For their belief in us, that our stories are part of the war that has never been told, we are forever grateful.

—Susan Johnson Hadler

Ann Mix also wishes to thank the following: Lorin McCleary for helping us find our publisher; the Helfgott family for their constant belief in this book and for lending us their home for our first work session; Anne Black, Walter Bellisi, Andrea, Andrina, and Franco who helped me learn my father's story; Bellingham friends who have been there in the sun and rain and watched and helped with a smile and a cheer: Linda Blackwell, Margaret Harwood Smith, Michaele Stephens, Carol Bartlett, John Servais, Bob Keller, Tom and Marilyn Junkersfeld, Phil Vandervelde, Jim Odell, Preston Taylor, Colleen Childers and Bob and Amy Walsh, friends Diana Glasgow and Trisha Leishman; and my family who brings me joy and loving comfort, always—Cydney, Seth, Serena, Chris, Ryan, Kevin, Wilder, Dana, Terri, Cindi and Anne.

—Ann Bennett Mix

INDEX

243